THEY CAME WITH COURAGE

COLIN PRICE

QAWRA PRESS

By the same author

They Came to a Country

First published by Qawra Press 2004

Copyright © Colin Price

All rights reserved. No part of this publication may be reproduced, stored in a retrieval system or transmitted in any form or by any means, electronic, mechanical, photocopying, recording or otherwise, without prior written permission of the publisher, nor be otherwise circulated in any form of binding or cover other than that in which it is published and without a similar condition including this being imposed on the subsequent purchaser.

Price, Colin Huntley, 1932-.
They came with courage.

ISBN 0-9752196-0-X

1.Spouses of clergy - Western Australia - Fiction. 2. Farm life - Western Australia - Fiction. 1. Title.

A823.4

Cover painting by Judith Magill

Typeset in Palatino by Color Logic

Printed and bound by Success Print
7a Goongarrie Street,
Bayswater. WA 6053
Australia

Qawra Press
66 Northmore Crescent
Winthrop WA 6150
Australia
Ph/Fax (08) 9310 3132

ABOUT THE AUTHOR

Born in London, Colin Price was brought up on a farm on the coast of East Anglia and educated in Britain. He came to Australia aged sixteen and spent the first nine years on sheep and cattle stations in the Northwest of Western Australia. He joined a Pastoral House and for the next twenty-three years was involved in all aspects of their business, including eleven years in East Asia and Europe. Following his early retirement he has been farming in the Avon Valley.

Acknowledgements

My thanks go to Judith Magill for her painting of "The Old Rectory" which forms the basis of the front cover of this book.

To Trudy Graham, Sally Hincks, Adelphe and Walter King for reviewing the final draft and their constructive comments.

To Beryl Hailes for her supportive editing and patience.

To Margaret for her support and enthusiasm for this project.

My gratitude goes to Jeff Dittrich for his advice and skill in bringing this novel to fruition.

To Ada Mary, a true pioneer.

Author's Note

Throughout this work I have endeavoured to strictly apply the formula of placing the fictional characters with the occasional historical figure into an authentic setting.
Colin Price

CHAPTER 1
March 1890

"I tell you Ellen, I will not allow these girls to read rubbish like this on the Lord's Day. This is what happens when you go to the Minster church. You should keep to our own class at the chapel."

Martha Hayward gently closed the door to cut off the sound of her father's voice and walked quietly to the hallstand.

Why does father always disapprove of what we read? She thought.

"Now Joseph," her mother had said so patiently at the breakfast table. "I don't think the vicar implied any criticism of you when he spoke of the responsibilities of employers to their employees when times are bad. He certainly doesn't blame you when men are dismissed at the mill. Everyone knows you are only the manager at Brodie & Pike's and it is George Brodie who tells you how many men to put off."

Her mother's statement hadn't calmed her father, who was sensitive to any suggestion that he was not in control of the small woollen mill at the lower end of the town.

He is always angry, she thought, if not with mother for being the daughter of Elwyn Jones, the solicitor, then with Ailine for being clever, or with me because I go to church with mother at the Minster. He knows I don't like the chapel at Dilton Marsh and I hate it when he preaches there, particularly when he shouts at the congregation from the pulpit. Father is so resentful that grandfather Jones insisted that Ailine and I had as much right to a good education as our brother Tom and paid our school fees.

Martha shrugged into her topcoat, then put on her hat and secured it to her thick chestnut hair with a large hatpin. She went to the door and let herself into the street where the cold

March wind tugged at her skirts as it swirled along Portway.

I can't bear this place, she thought, as she turned away from the house. She caught sight of her sister hurrying towards her on the other side of the street and crossed over to wait for Ailine to come up to her.

"Where are you going, Martha?"

Martha shrugged indifferently. "I don't know. Wherever I can get away from Father. He found the book you were reading this morning and threatened to burn it. He's hateful and I can't bear him shouting at Mother about our friends at the Minster."

Ailine looked more perplexed than upset. "But what would Father find to object to in John Stuart Mill? After all it was Canon Phillips who lent me the book after I told him that I had been reading The Wealth of Nations."

"He said it's rubbish."

"But Martha, it's an old book that is used at Oxford, not as old as Adam Smith's perhaps - that was written in 1776 - he usually approves of anything old!"

Martha looked at the serious young face in front of her and wondered how her sister could fail to understand that their father had a rigid objection to them reading any book other than the Bible on a Sunday. The trouble is, she thought, Allie slips through life with her nose buried in her books and her mind in the clouds.

"I'm going for a walk up to Arndown and back. Father wasn't aware that I was in the house and Mrs Joiner won't have dinner ready for another hour. That was another thing that he was shouting at Mother about, as though the most important thing in the world was for us all to go down to the chapel and hear him preach this afternoon."

"I'll come with you," decided Ailine.

The two girls started to walk towards the chalk ridge that overlooked the town.

Ailine quickly forgot about her father's annoyance at her choice of books and gave her sister a resume of her activities that morning at Sunday School, where she had helped with the little ones as an assistant teacher.

Martha listened with part of her mind and provided sufficient monosyllabic replies to maintain the conversational flow while she thought of her own morning and her attendance with her mother at Holy Communion. Her mother had been brought up in Warminster and had always attended the parish church. While obedient to her husband's wishes in most matters, she remained adamant that she would continue to worship at the church of her childhood, the church her father still attended, where Canon Sir James Erasmus Phillips had been vicar for many years.

Martha recalled the look she had exchanged with the handsome, vaguely saturnine curate, Robert Gladwell, as she had accepted the chalice from his hands at the altar rail. She wondered whether he had seen her love for him, as she had seen love in his eyes. Her father would never have approved of that.

She became aware of Ailine repeatedly asking a question and came back to earth.

"I am sorry, Allie. I didn't hear what you said. I was thinking of something else."

"I said, shouldn't we be going home now? We'll be late for lunch."

Martha looked about her and seeing the downs stretching away to the east realised to her horror that they were into the next valley, out of sight of the town.

"Oh!" she gasped, her hand to her mouth. "We must have been walking for ages. We'll have to dash." She turned and set off down the narrow lane towards their home with her sister running to keep up.

They entered the house and found their mother in the morning room. She looked up as they entered the room and said serenely, "Your father has been called to the mill. There's something amiss at the dye house. We are to keep his meal warm until he returns."

Martha looked at the black marble mantle clock above the fireplace. "If he is not home soon," she replied tartly, "he'll not have time to eat before going off to the chapel. Then he'll be in an even worse mood than he was when I went out."

"Martha, I will not have you speak disparagingly of your father," her mother spoke sharply. She lowered her voice and addressed her younger daughter. "Ailine, would you please tell Mrs Joiner that we won't wait and would she bring the meal to the dining room. Would you help her, please."

Ailine left the room and Mrs Hayward pushed her needle into her tapestry and setting the frame aside, stood up. She looked at the determined figure of her elder daughter and smiled.

"Martha, it isn't wise to take life's setbacks head on. You must learn to compromise. I am well aware that you are upset that your father doesn't wish you to encourage Mr Gladwell's attentions. You understand very well why he doesn't approve of you forming a connection with Church of England clergy. However, I know that Mr Gladwell comes of a good family. Given time your father will come about, if you will only be patient and not rush your fences."

"But Mother, Robert has been most proper and conducted himself exactly as he should, asking father for his permission to call and everything. It was only when he told father that he had responded to the letter in the "Church Times" from that bishop in Western Australia seeking the assistance of young clergymen, that he became so difficult."

"Martha, your father is only concerned for your own good. He is quite right; it is not fitting that you should go out to Australia until Mr Gladwell is established. It is undoubtedly still quite primitive on the West Australian Goldfields. The miners are mostly Irish, or so I am led to believe, and everyone knows that they live like savages. I remember only too well my father's description of the terrible conditions in the camps that the Irish navigators lived in when they were building the Kennet and Avon Canal. If Mr Gladwell goes out to the colony, you could follow him later when he has a home ready for you and could marry him there."

"Oh Mother! Do you really think I could? I thought father had set his mind completely against Robert," Martha said in a rush.

Mrs Hayward sighed. "When Mrs Gladwell visited us recently, your dear father was very taken with her. She told him that she planned to accompany her younger son and his wife to West Australia, just as soon as he has completed his articles as a solicitor. I don't think your father will object to you travelling with their party when the time comes. Appearances can be deceptive, Martha. If you will have a little patience and show proper respect to your father, I have no doubt we will contrive. Now let us go into luncheon and later we will go with your father to Dilton Marsh and listen to him preach." She led the way to the door and along the hall to the dining room.

The problem at the dye house took longer to resolve than Joseph Hayward had expected and when he finally returned to the house in Portway it was only to wash his hands and to change into his best suit before pedalling rapidly away on his bicycle.

As a result Martha was able to persuade her mother that she and Ailine should take a walk along George Street and the Bath Road to the Minster, in time for the evening service.

Ailine was inside the church out of the wind and Martha in the porch when Robert Gladwell came up the cobbled path in his cassock, his surplice thrown over an arm.

Seeing Martha on the stone bench within the porch, he stopped and addressed her excitedly. "I have great news! The Bishop of Perth has replied offering me a living."

"Oh!" Martha enthused. "That is wonderful. Tell me about it."

"I am to be the Rector of Bolumbygine, a country parish covering several hundred square miles, with seven churches."

"But isn't that rather a lot for one man to look after on his own? Won't you have a curate to help you, Robert?"

"No. The Bishop has written that since the discovery of gold there has been a substantial increase in the population and as a result they are very short-handed. There are only sixteen ordained parish priests to serve a population approaching two hundred thousand, and he is expecting that the eight men he has now appointed will make a big difference. He is making arrangements for a berth for me on a Peninsula and Orient Line steamer as soon as he can."

"What about me, Robert? Will you ask father if we may be married?"

Robert regarded her fondly. "Why not? After all, I now have a living and will require a wife to assist me in the parochial work. My father left me a small bequest to allow me some comfort once I am called to my first parish. The executors of his estate can hardly refuse to pay it to me now. Your father will be pleased about this aspect, being in trade and all that. I will, after all, be well able to keep you in the style to which you have been accustomed," he added sententiously.

Martha put her disquiet at his manner aside and, leaping to her feet, threw her arms around the young man's neck and hugged him. Robert disengaged himself from her embrace and looked quickly around to make sure that they had not been observed.

"Martha," he said, "it is not the done thing to give way to one's feelings in public. You must be more decorous. I have a position to keep up, you know. People will look to us to set the standard in the future."

Martha could forgive him anything at this moment, even his stuffiness. "Oh, Robert," she breathed, her eyes shining. "you will make a wonderful missionary, preaching to all those Australian Aborigines."

"You are not quite right there," admonished her beloved. "I have been told that few of the original inhabitants have survived the diseases the white man brought with him, measles, scarlet fever and so on, against which they had little natural resistance."

Martha wrinkled her forehead as she recalled her mother's comment about the camps for the railway workers.

"Will most of your parishioners be farmers or miners? Mother said there may be a lot of Irish immigrants working in the gold mines."

Robert spread his hands. "It will be a great challenge. The Bishop has written that most of the members of the church in our parish are descendants of the free settlers who originally went out to take up agricultural land. They make up only a small proportion of the colony's population, many of whom are Wesleyans and other dissenters. Quite a number were originally convicts, often Roman Catholics of Irish descent, sent to the Swan River Colony from this country in the 1850's at the request of the early settlers to help clear the land for farming."

"I know about that," Martha said. "My grandfather Hayward, the one who was a lock keeper on the Kennet and Avon Canal, told me that when the agricultural labourers, who were arrested during the riots here in Wiltshire and Dorset fifty years ago, were brought before the bench, the first thing the magistrates wanted to know was whether the prisoners were chapel people or Catholics. He said that it was rough justice and Botany Bay for any who admitted it."

Robert looked at her for a moment.

"I don't think you should repeat that criticism of the magistrates, Martha. My grandfather was a magistrate in Hampshire and would have been scrupulously fair. We ought to go in now, it's almost time."

He turned, opened the door into the church and stood back to let her enter.

****

Chapter 2

Waiting

May

Martha lay in her bed and stared at the ceiling of her small room as she reviewed the events of the previous day. In spite of the emotion that she had experienced when she had said goodbye to Robert at the railway station, she had enjoyed the attention of the little group of people who had come to see him off.

The Vicar had been kind and had twinkled when he said that she wouldn't be too far behind Robert. Some of the women had looked at her queerly, as though to say, why aren't you getting married now and going out to the colonies as man and wife. The truth was that she didn't mind now that she was officially engaged to Robert and would go out to him next year, when he had a home ready for her. In the meantime she would be sewing for her trousseau. Her grandfather had already given her money towards this and had told her to make sure that she had a dozen of everything, as it was most unlikely she would be able to buy such things as sheets and tablecloths, let alone Witney blankets, in Australia. She smiled to herself; he really was a dear.

She had seen girls in the congregation looking at her these last few weeks with envy in their eyes as she had waited after morning service for Robert to escort her home for Sunday luncheon. Dear Robert, he was so different from the other men in the town or from the surrounding villages. Always so courteous and correct, he had even asked her permission before kissing her the first time. His kisses she now knew could become fiercely passionate and on occasion rouse her to the point that she almost lost control of herself. Yet it was always Robert who pulled away from her and left her with a feeling of frustration that nothing could assuage.

Her girl friends at school had whispered to each other that men always wanted to touch a girl in ways that were not discussed amongst nice people. She could remember going to a ball at the Town Hall and she had taken fright when Billy Greville had taken her aside in the dark and had touched her bosom while he kissed her wetly on the lips. She smiled to herself in the half-light of early morning. At the time she had felt soiled by the experience and yet afterwards had wondered what would have happened if she had let Billy go further. She frowned. Robert had never made any attempt to touch her or in anyway given her reason to rebuff his advances, which of course she would have done she told herself.

There had been one time on Copheap Hill when she had thought he was going to initiate something. She had kissed him lingeringly and in response he had crushed her to him, but almost before she had realised what was happening he had pushed her away from him and, turning, had looked out over the town for several minutes. Then he had taken her hand and they had continued along the path that led across the hill. Robert talked quietly all the while about the responsibility that would be placed upon them to lead the people of their parish. While Martha listened with only half her attention, she wondered whether she had just missed something exciting.

She heard the sound of a sheep bell, followed by the rippling patter of small hooves as a flock of sheep from off the plain passed down the street towards the market in the centre of the town. The occasional bleat of a sheep gave way to the shouts of the shepherds as they urged the flock along, to be followed by the sound of a horse's hoofs and the crunch of steel shod wheels as a wagon came up from George Street and headed towards Westbury.

A knock came at the door of her bedroom and her mother entered. "My, you are a lazybones this morning, Martha," she said, looking about her. "There is a lot to do today and before you know where you are Mrs Gladwell will be writing to say she is ready to leave for the antipodes and you won't have all your things in your box."

Martha sat up. "Oh Mother!" she said, "that won't be until next year."

"You'll be surprised how quickly time passes. Mrs Gladwell has written inviting you to stay at Winchester. You will need some dresses to be made for you by then."

September

The sun glinted on the river as it flowed around the buttressed stone piers of the acquaduct that carried the canal in arched splendour over road, river and rail. Swirling slowly away, the water rested in the millpond above the weir then rushed through the millrace in turbulent joy before cascading into the pool on the other side of the fulling mill.

Martha sat on the stone wall and listened to the cries of the children on the Sunday School picnic as they played under their teachers' eyes in the meadow above.

It was peaceful sitting under the old limes in front of the "Crossed Guns" as she imagined the mill-hands would sit in the late evening and drink their beer.

Taking out Robert's letter from where it was concealed in the front of her black waistband, she unfolded the pages, aware that though she had only received it the week before the paper was beginning to tear along the folds. She wrinkled her nose and wondered whether it would be better to make a fair copy to carry with her to read in private and leave the original in the box on the chest of drawers in her bedroom where she kept her most precious things. Straightening it, she started to read.

"The bishop was not able to see me the first day of our arrival in Perth. His secretary met us at the railway station. A most able man, like my father, he is a Wykamist and an Oxford man to boot. He was at New College and seemed to know several of the dons who were there in my time. We had a nice chat as he took our small party of newcomers sightseeing in a Hansom cab.

The town overlooks a series of wide lagoons through which the Swan River flows. It is situated about ten miles upstream from Fremantle where many of the first settlers landed, though it is at Albany some two hundred and fifty miles to the south that the mail ships now call on their way to Eastern Australia. Perth is a surprisingly substantial place with several large buildings along St Georges Terrace, the main thoroughfare. However, there is an air of colonialism as, even in the main street, there are private houses with wide verandahs and corrugated iron roofs. Away from the centre of the town the houses are for the most part single storey, but here and there are quite large two storey houses with well tended gardens of semitropical plants including many palm trees.

My companions are no doubt well meaning men, but not exactly the quality I would have myself chosen to represent the church here in the antipodes. They are however a far better type of person than those I met when the bishop introduced us to the clergy attending the meeting of the diocesan synod. Without in anyway being uncharitable, I was quite surprised to find that many of the clergy indulge themselves excessively, even drinking alcoholic spirits during the day rather than the occasional sherry before dinner. I was very much amused by the names of the country towns many of which ended in "Up". Dinninup, Dwellingup, Tambleup and Nannup come to mind. There was even a place called Wyalkatchem, at least that is how I think it is spelt.

I will be going to York very soon where I am to be introduced to my new parishioners and will then make a tour of my parish. I believe it is larger in extent than Wiltshire and though there are several small towns and villages in this vast area, they are scattered sometimes twenty or more miles apart.

At first I will be boarding with a Mr and Mrs Robinson at Bolumbygine but once I have settled to my work, I will set in hand the building of a suitable rectory, so as to have everything ready for you when you come out with mother.

Please give my felicitations to your parents. I will write again as soon as I have more news.

Yours truly, Robert Gladwell"

Martha sighed and folded the letter again. It was a pity that Robert had not written to say how much he missed her and that he could not wait to have her with him. She frowned and pursed her lips as she looked down at the grubby little wedge of folded paper lying in her hands. She wrote him such loving letters every week, telling him what she had been doing and how much she missed him. She sat deep in thought then, with a shrug abruptly stood, thrust the letter into her waist band, and picked up her parasol from where she had placed it against the stone wall.

As she turned there was a flash of blue along the river as two kingfishers flew low over the water. They darted over the weir and across the millpond past the old fulling mill down to where the weaving mill's race spilled its water back into the main stream. Then, to her joy, they came back along the nearer bank and passed into the shade of the arches of the acquaduct.

The steam whistle of the small pleasure craft split the air, calling the Sunday School party aboard, to be taken back to Bradford-upon-Avon where they would join the railway train that would take them home. She set off up the slight rise to the canal where the others were gathering.

Later, sitting on the foredeck of the little steamboat with two sleepy children lying beside her, another child's head in her lap, Martha marvelled at the varied green of the trees stretching up the hillside above the canal. The beeches and ash trees rose, tier upon tier, to the puffballs of cloud that were forming in the sky. Behind her the steam engine hissed and wheezed, quietly thumping as its pistons drove them slowly along under the canopy of entwined branches. Surely, she thought, there are not many places in the world as peaceful or beautiful as Wiltshire in autumn. The child in her lap stirred and turned on her side. Martha smiled happily as she gently pushed a damp curl back from the little girl's face.

****

Chapter 3

1892 Albany, West Australia

Martha followed Robert's mother onto the promenade deck of the Peninsula and Orient Line steamship. There she found that the low sandhills of the landfall they had made the previous evening, had changed to purple scrub covered hills falling down to sun-etched grey rock edged with the white lace of the sea.

The morning sun shone from behind her as they steamed steadily up the expanse of King George Sound towards the pair of granite hills that guard the narrow entrance channel to Princess Royal Harbour and the town of Albany.

"Why it's lovely!" she cried. "The air is so clear and there isn't a cloud in the sky."

"It is certainly a lovely day. Robert said in his letters that there is no lack of sunlight in Australia." Emily Gladwell looked around the deck for her younger son. "There's William!" She pointed towards the area under the bridge.

He was standing looking forward towards the bow where a small group of seamen had gathered to prepare for the vessel's entrance to the harbour. Hearing her cry he turned and seeing the two women hurried towards them.

"You're up early Mother! You too Martha. One of the officers told me that we ought to be alongside within the hour. Have you had breakfast?"

"Yes, we have," his mother replied. "Elizabeth was going in to the dining saloon as we came away. She looked quite sick, poor girl, which is understandable at this time."

"It may well be, hopefully, once we are ashore she will be better. Isn't it a beautiful day? A good omen. I think Papa would have liked this, Mother."

He smiled at them both and made his way below deck to join his young wife.

Robert Gladwell looked up at the side of the mail ship as, aided by a steam tug, it came alongside the Albany jetty. He had seen the group of figures at the rail almost as soon as the vessel had negotiated the narrow entrance into Princess Royal Harbour. Now he was able to identify Martha in her cornflower blue dress, a wide brimmed straw hat to protect her face from the morning sun, standing beside his mother. He waved to them, before checking himself, as he doubted it was appropriate for a man of the cloth to wave in public.

Within minutes the accommodation gangway was lowered to the jetty and he was able to make his way on board. There he greeted his mother, brother and sister-in-law, and then strangely ill at ease, turned to the young woman who had travelled twelve thousand miles to become his wife. She regarded him quizzically from under the brim of her hat and looking into her eyes he felt a wave of emotion that left him breathless.

Emily Gladwell drew William and Elizabeth to one side; her elder son and his intended wife were in any case oblivious to them.

Tears started to grow in Martha's eyes and, welling over, coursed down her cheeks as she looked at Robert. He was more careworn than the man she had bade farewell to a year and a half before, but a man who seemed to have gained in confidence and whose hands bore the evidence of hard physical work.

He took a step towards her and taking her into his arms kissed her, knocking her hat off.

Emily had watched the pair of them from the corner of her eye as she talked lightly to William and Elizabeth by the ship's rail. Her eyes narrowed as she saw her son's quick movement towards Martha then widened in surprise at the passionate embrace. She moved towards them, her hand raised to arrest Robert's impetuous action. However, William stepped in front of her before she could intervene.

"Mother," he warned, smiling at her. "I think we should go down now and ask the cabin steward to bring the remainder of our luggage up. I expect Robert will have made arrangements for accommodation at an hotel until our train leaves for Perth."

His mother was scandalised. "Robert is a priest," she whispered sibilantly, "he shouldn't behave like that in public. Your father would never have allowed it."

He slipped his hand under her arm and taking his wife's hand, bore them both off, saying as he did so, "Just behave as though nothing has happened. Please don't embarrass them now; they'll be shocked enough in retrospect later."

Martha and Robert were quite unaware of the consternation they had caused and were standing quietly, their arms around each other, her head on his shoulder.

"I have arranged for us to be married today so that we may travel directly to our new home. I thought it would be wiser, but now I wonder if I am rushing you too much." He looked down at her. "I have arranged with Mr Strelley for the ceremony to be at four this afternoon. If you would rather leave it until tomorrow, please tell me."

She leaned back in his arms and looked into his eyes as she considered his statement then smiled. "My wedding dress is in the top of my trunk. Having just experienced your welcome, I think it would be best if we were married today."

She withdrew gently from his arms and turned to pick up her hat from the deck. Extending her hand to him she said, "Come Robert, we have to get ready and I am just longing to go home tomorrow."

It was a hot night and Martha lay under the mosquito netting on her back, her hands clasped under her head, her legs apart like a starfish, listening to Robert's breathing beside her.

It hadn't been too bad, she mused. In fact, once she had got over the shock of Robert's need for her, she had enjoyed it. By that time she had an almost overwhelming need for him too and it had been a relief to find that all the dreadful stories she had heard from her school friends were untrue. Certainly she was quite pleased that she had managed things so well. In retrospect however she was a little surprised to find that Robert had so rapidly lost interest in her and had rolled over and gone off to sleep, leaving her awake and ready to continue. She smiled. Who were the stronger of the species? Females of course.

A cool breeze lifted the mosquito netting, cooling her skin. She shivered and, sliding her legs over the side of the bed, picked up her night dress from under the pillow where she had pushed it, ducked out from under the netting and slipped the sheer silk over her head.

It was quiet on the verandah overlooking the harbour as she carefully opened the French door. She turned and picked up her dressing gown from the end of the bed and stepped outside. Light from the full moon fell on the boats anchored in the wide expanse before her. Nearby on the verandah was an old rocking chair with turned rails to the seat and arms that she remembered having seen when they had first arrived at the hotel. Painted battleship grey, and with its seat covered by a piece of old carpet, it had seen happier days.

Putting on her gown she sank gratefully onto the rocker and was surprised how comfortable it was. It creaked gently as it moved under her weight, seeming to welcome her. She sat listening to the night sounds as she looked at the scene before her.

A door slammed below and a man came out from the verandah that ran across the front of the hotel. He was joined by another, taller man, the light shining on his blonde hair.

One of them spoke: "Arthur, did you see the sheila that married that priest today?"

"Nao. What did she look like?"

"Pretty little thing, big eyes, red hair."

Peering over the edge of the verandah from the shadows above, Martha flushed.

"Good legs?" asked his mate.

"Dunno. I'm not much of a legs man meself. But I tell you what."

"Well, what?"

"Bloody waste, married to a priest. He wouldn't know what to do with her."

"Nao, s'pose not. But he wasn't a Mick, that's for sure. Don't allow them to marry do they? Probably one of them Methodists, they always have dozens of kids."

The other man was silent for a while. "Are you coming to turn in now, Arthur?"

"Nao Bill. But you gave me an idea. I'll go an' get a bottle o'beer from the landlord, if he's still up, an' take it around to that barmaid's room, around the back."

"You're a glutton for punishment. I thought you had enough of her last night to last a lifetime. Well, see yer in the mornin'."

"Yeah, see yer."

They moved out of earshot.

Martha rocked herself gently and smiled to herself. After a while she stood up and moved quietly through the bedroom, past her husband now sprawled on his back and snoring gently. She opened the door into the passage and walked to the bathroom.

Coming back she took a wrong turn and found herself in the full light of the moon on the back verandah of the hotel. She paused and looked across the town at the hills above. As she turned to re-enter the building she became aware of a man leaning against the wall beside the door. Two eyes under a shock of blonde hair stared straight at her.

Startled, she threw her hands up. "Oh, you surprised me!" she said. "I didn't see you in the shadows there."

"Nao, but I saw you, looked right purty too, standing there with the light from that moon shining through your dress."

She was taken aback by this statement. "Oh!" she exclaimed. "You horrid man."

"Nao, not horrible. Appreciative, that's what I am." He slurred his words slightly, which increased her agitation. "What about a bedtime kiss, love."

He stood away from the wall and, reaching out to her arms, pulled her towards him.

Martha received the beer fumes full in her face and stepped back instinctively, fighting the strong hands that pulled her forward. Recalling her days in the schoolyard, she relaxed and pretended to go limp. The man loosened his grip slightly. Immediately she brought her knee up sharply between his legs. Grunting, he sagged forward and as his head came down she grasped his hair and stepping to one side pulled him off balance and smashed his head into the verandah post behind her. His knees buckled and groaning he crumpled to the floor. Martha didn't wait to see whether he was badly hurt and ran through the doorway into the hotel and back to her room. Once inside, she shot the bolt and stood with her back to the door, panting.

After a while she became aware that Robert was still in the same position as when she left him, breathing quietly. She was tempted to awaken him and tell him what had happened, but thinking better of it slipped out of her dressing gown and turning her husband on his side slid into bed.

Lying back, she smiled in the dark, then feeling weary, closed her eyes.

****

Chapter 4

Bolumbygine

The offside horse blew flecks of foam from its mouth as it crossed the river. It raised its head and with ears pricked snorted in satisfaction as it recognised where it was.

Robert gathered the reins into his left hand and lifted his low crowned hat, the livid mark of the sweatband gleaming above his dark eyes. He glanced at his young wife of two days, sitting beside him. She showed no hint of fatigue after the long train trip north from Albany to the terminus of the recently completed Great Southern Railway line at Beverley.

There he had left his mother, brother and sister-in-law, who had arranged to stay overnight at the hotel in the main street before travelling onward on the West Australian Government Railway to Perth. Having wished them well, he had secured his horses and buggy from the rear of the Settlers Arms and set out with Martha for Bolumbygine an hour to the west of the small township.

"Not much further to go now, Martha," he said kindly. "We'll be home well before dark and I'll light the fire. We can cook some of the meat that Mrs Fogarty gave us."

"I do wish your mother had agreed to come and stay with us," Martha said. "I feel awful about her going on to Perth straight away with William and Elizabeth."

"Mother sees her first task is to support William in taking up his position with Cowan, Dibney and West. Once he has joined the practice and they have a house, then Mother may feel able to come and stay with us." He smiled, "Mother would never buy a house she hadn't seen herself. It is her money, not William's, and she will have very definite views as to what is suitable."

Martha looked around her. She had found the mile upon mile of low scrub and trees vaguely disturbing in its sameness during the journey north from Albany, whereas here the increasingly large gum trees and dense thickets of raspberry jam trees all seemed to indicate more fertile land. Robert had explained to her that the coastal plain that extended north and south of the Swan River, where the colony had been established in 1829, was largely made up of deep white sands, which had proved relatively infertile. Similarly the gravels of the Darling Ranges that paralleled the coast for four hundred miles appeared only suitable to support the eucalypt hardwood forests. These forests produced the magnificently durable Jarrah or Swan River Mahogany used for furniture and the wood blocks used to surface major streets in the City of London and also the lighter coloured Blackbutt and, perhaps the ultimate in hardwoods, the white barked Wandoo.

He had told her of the difficulties faced by the little settlement and how it had nearly foundered in the first years of colonisation, until two events occurred. First the expedition led by Ensign Dale to the east over the Darling Ranges in 1830, had discovered the fertile soils of the Avon Valley. Then twenty years later the Colonial Office in London had agreed to the settlers's request to provide them with cheap labour from British prisons.

The four-wheeled buggy, the pair of horses harnessed to its single pole, swung around the corner in the track at the top of the river's bank.

Through the trees Martha could see signs of farming, the land cleared and a crop of ripening wheat waving in the light wind. As the track wound away from the riverbank they passed a house with its outbuildings set back from the road under the trees, then another on the other side.

"That's the Robinson's place," said Robert, indicating the house on the right and slightly above the road, "where I have been going for the evening meal, when I am here on a Sunday.

Mr Robinson was the main supporter of the project to build the church at Bolumbygine ten years ago. Over there is the Sievright's house; they are good people too. Further to the north is Broughton Park, which is the largest property around here. It has been owned by the Webb family ever since land was first taken up in the Avon Valley in the early thirties." He frowned and fell silent.

The buggy had climbed a long slope as Robert talked and straight ahead, through the trees, Martha caught sight of a small church with a high gabled roof. Built of the local stone it sat on the hillside, its roof of sheoak shingles almost silver in colour, and two dark green sheoak trees stood in front of its low porch.

"Why Robert, it's charming," she exclaimed. "How many people does it seat?"

"Thirty six. You must realise that while St Margaret's in the Valley is the smallest of the churches in my parish it is situated in the prettiest location of them all. There's the rectory behind it, to the left." Reining in the horses he brought the buggy to a halt.

Martha looked in dismay at the simple building that was to be her home. It was typical of the time and the country, the design strongly influenced by the bungalows occupied by British Colonial Officials in India. It was built of stone with a corrugated iron roof and stood foursquare facing south. At the back, the house was protected by a wide bullnose verandah of corrugated iron that had been curved tightly by passing it through the rollers of a curving machine. This process strengthened each sheet at the eaves end to allow the verandah to be spanned economically without the use of rafters and midspaced purlins.

She compared the small building on the bare hillside with the substantial vicarages in the rural parishes of Wiltshire, and was shocked. It's tiny! she thought.

Putting her disappointment aside, she turned to Robert and

said quietly. "Robert, it will be beautiful once we have planted a garden and have some flowers and trees. It's a lovely position and we will be able to look over the river and along the valley to the hills."

Sensing her unspoken disappointment, he said nothing and urged the horses up the hill towards the house. Coming to the crest of the hill he pointed to the small hay shed where he stored the feed for the horses and the adjoining thatch roofed bush shelter where, he explained, the buggy stood out of the sun.

As he pulled up at the back verandah, Robert passed the reins to Martha and springing from the buggy undid the ropes securing their baggage on the tray behind the seat.

"I don't know why you wanted to buy that old rocking chair from the hotel in Albany," he grumbled, as he untied the knot in the last of the ropes and took the offending piece of furniture down.

Martha said nothing but held the reins lightly in her hands until he had unloaded the smaller pieces of baggage to the ground. Robert moved to the horses' heads and, grasping the bit of the nearside animal, held them as she climbed down from the buggy and stood looking around her. Her nostrils flared as she became aware of the unfamiliar aroma of dry dust, horse sweat, gum leaves and distant wood smoke.

"Take your valise into the house, Martha, the door isn't locked. Ted Robinson will be up before long, with some milk. When he comes I'll ask him to help me carry in your steamer trunk."

Martha picked up the small carpetbag that contained the things that she needed overnight, noticing as she did so that there were trails of ants everywhere on the ground.

She stepped deliberately over the ant trails as she walked to the verandah. A large tabby cat picked itself up from the gunnysack that was serving as a mat in front of the door and stalked leisurely away, its back arched stiffly, its tail erect, flagging its disdain of the intruder. Martha's heels clattered on the hard boards as, crossing the verandah, she made for the unpainted door.

Entering the house she found herself in the kitchen, which, though sparsely furnished with a scrubbed deal table and three windsor chairs, was well provided with shelves along one wall and a large iron woodstove in the fireplace.

The fire in the stove was laid and putting her bag and her hat on the table, Martha took down a tin of wax vestas from the mantelpiece. She extracted a match, struck it on the side of the tin and thrust it flaring into the little wigwam of leaves and sticks. The tinder dry gum leaves caught immediately, giving off a pleasant scent, and the small twigs crackled merrily as the chimney started to draw.

Martha immediately felt less strange and, standing straight backed, turned and looked about her. It was a well lit room with a box sash sliding window beside the chimney and another looking towards the sheds. Both windows could do with curtains, she thought. The floor of dark red boards was bare of any covering and was clean apart from a light film of reddish dust. A few items of cheap crockery were on the shelves and some iron pots sat on the hob beside the stove. A large tin bowl was propped on its edge against the wall under the window beside the fireplace.

Looking through the window and across the verandah to the shed she could see that Robert had unharnessed both horses and was brushing one of them down.

Martha turned away and opened the door into the next room at the rear of the house, which was empty except for a small iron framed bed. Disappointed, she closed the door and explored further. The front room was furnished with two unmatched chairs; one a plush covered upright chair with wings, the other a small leather chair with a round back. There was no other furniture in the room except for a small six sided table made of the same hardwood that comprised the floors and other woodwork in the house, but which had been sanded smooth and waxed to bring out a fine figured grain. She stopped beside the little table and ran her hand over it. It was cool and smooth to her touch.

The front door opened into this room and beside it was the door to the fourth and last room. Martha opened this and peered in. It was dark and the curtains were drawn across the windows. Nevertheless there was sufficient light for her to see a large brass double bed that stood with its head against the inside wall, its foot facing south and a pair of chests of drawers standing one on either side of the window on the east side. There was no wardrobe, or hanging space, except that a frame had been built to take a hanging rail across the corner of the room beside the head of the bed. Robert's cassock and black worsted suits were neatly hung in the space provided.

She returned to the kitchen, picked up her hat and bag and carried them into the bedroom. From the bag she took a comb and ran it through her thick hair before making her way back to the kitchen where the kettle was now singing softly. She passed through onto the verandah and found Robert, stripped to the waist, washing in a bowl on a dilapidated washstand. She stood looking at his finely muscled back and shoulders as he sluiced water over his face and neck. With his eyes tightly shut and his hands reaching out before him, he started across the verandah towards an old chair against the wall on which was hung a towel. Missing the back of the chair he stumbled over it and nearly fell. Martha recovered the towel and placed it in his hand. He opened his eyes cautiously, glanced at the towel and recognising what it was, shut his eyes again and wiped the soapy water off his face.

She smiled at him and moved rapidly across the verandah, where she washed her hands and face in the bowl before throwing the water out.

"Is there a bathroom, Robert?" she asked, as she took the towel from him and dried her face and hands.

"I was thinking of making one off the verandah here at the back, or perhaps near our bedroom. Then I ran out of money and thought it better to await your arrival before making a decision. The biggest problem at the moment is the shortage of water. We have to cart it from the Robinson's well down the hill. If we could have a rainwater tank built before next winter we could collect the water from the roof. This would give us plenty for drinking and we would only have to cart water for the washing and so on."

She regarded him with amazement. "Didn't you think of water before building the house? Surely it was more likely you would find water down by the river?"

Holding his shirt in his hands, he looked at her apprehensively then shrugged his shoulders. "I wanted to build the rectory near the church where there was a pleasant view. I thought we could pipe in water from the river later. It is well drained up here and I thought that was important, as we didn't want a damp house, not like my parents' home in England. You must agree," he added persuasively, "it was necessary to be near the church. In any case Fred Sievright didn't want to sell me any land down by the river. He was however, willing to let me have this land on the hill beside the church."

"I have no doubt he was very happy to let you have this stony ridge," she said tartly, looking at him pityingly, then returned to the kitchen.

They had just sat down at the table to hot weak black tea when there was a step on the verandah and a knock on the door. Martha jumped up and flew to straighten her hair.

She returned from her bedroom to find a big man with a drooping black moustache, thick greying hair and piercing blue eyes sitting at the table with Robert.

"This is Mr Robinson, Martha." Robert said, as the man stood up awkwardly.

"Pleased to meet you Mrs Gladwell," he said, standing behind his chair like a small schoolboy. "Edith sent me up with the milk and some bread to tide you over until you have time to bake tomorrow. I fetched the cow back as I thought you'd like to milk her yourself in the morning. Brought some cooked mutton up too and some chops for breakfast. I know the Reverend has a few old ewes for killers down the paddock, but you'd not have time to kill one tonight."

"Thank you Mr Robinson, please thank your wife for her kind thought. It really is most generous of you both. Will you sit down and have a cup of tea with us."

"No, thank you. I really shouldn't stay. Edith would have come herself but she is finding it difficult to get around just now. She asked that you please go down and see her just as soon as you are settled. Once we have had the happy event she is going to invite the neighbours over to meet you."

"Oh, that is kind. I thought I would probably meet everyone at church on Sunday."

"You will in time, but there are only the Sievrights and us that are C of E. The rest of the district either don't bother with church or go to the catholic church in York."

Robert looked up. "Martha, I haven't explained before, but the reason we are living here is that Bolumbygine is more or less the centre of the parish. My parishioners are scattered in little groups out on the farms. The majority of the people in the townships are descended from indentured servants and convicts. Many of the convicts who were sent here were men and women who had been a given a ticket of leave, as they were coming to the end of their sentence. They were permitted to take on labouring work with the larger landowners, or to set up in the country towns as blacksmiths, carpenters and the like."

Robinson nodded his agreement. "That's quite right, Rector. While convicts formed the gangs building bridges and government buildings in Perth and Fremantle, once they had completed the term of their sentence they were given a ticket of leave to obtain paid employment, many of them as shepherds in the days before the properties were fenced. Later they were permitted to take up conditional purchase land close to the farms on which they were employed for only pennies an acre, with the promise that they could have the freehold when part was cleared and fenced." He grinned; "It's not surprising perhaps, how quickly they built up a flock of their own, being the sort of people they were. Quite a few settled on their blocks and made a go of it. Of course with many of them being Irish and Catholic, they bred like rabbits." He apologised again.

Robert came to his rescue at this point and they talked of local matters for a while before he said goodbye and took himself off home.

As Robert came back from walking down to the road with Mr Robinson, he met Martha returning from the closet that had been built at some distance from the house.

"Robert, I was going to ask you why you had built the little house so far away from the main house, but having now experienced the flies I can see that you were very wise." She put her head on one side and looked at him. "We are pioneering aren't we?"

He smiled at her. "I am afraid so. I don't think there is a water closet anywhere outside Perth or Albany. I have become so used to the primitive sanitary arrangements that I no longer think about it. I am sorry. You were not brought up to these conditions."

She smiled. "Oh, don't you worry, that is the least of our problems. I have had plenty of experience of earth closets in the villages around Warminster and even some of the houses in the town. Why down at New Town most cottages still have cess pits or rely on the nightcart. Mother told me that when the town sewage was proposed a few years ago, everyone was very upset at the likely increase in the rates and that's why the sewage was only put in at our end of the town."

Robert frowned, and changed the subject abruptly. "I don't think we need to discuss the subject further as we are a long way from Warminster. Here, let me show you where I have been keeping the meat and other perishables," he said rapidly. He led her to the end of the verandah outside the kitchen, where there was a large wooden framed cupboard backing on to the house wall.

Martha looked at the cupboard closely. Its walls and the door were covered with perforated zinc sheet to allow the passage of air while excluding flies and other insects. The four legs of the cupboard stood in small tin trays of water to inhibit the entry of ants.

"This is the shaded side of the house and whatever wind we get can blow freely around the cupboard to keep it cool," he said proudly. "It is quite secure from flies, cockroaches, ants, woodlice and the like."

"I think it's a wonderful idea," said Martha hurriedly. "Robert, I have just remembered that we were going to ask Mr Robinson to help you bring my heavy luggage into the house so that I could unpack."

Robert looked contrite. "It's a bit late for me to go down and ask him to come back now. Could we open it up where it is on the back of the buggy and then bring your things over from there?"

"Oh, don't worry Robert. They can stay there until the morning. I don't suppose it will rain." She glanced at the evening sky, where the sun was sinking rapidly to the west in a blaze of dark red, amber and gold.

****

CHAPTER 5
September 1893

Martha sat in the rocking chair on the front verandah of the rectory, her sewing in her hand as she waited for Robert to return from Narrogin.

Life in the West Australian bush was certainly different, she thought. In the last ten months much had been achieved in the garden. Fencing it off from the paddock surrounding the house had been a major step forward. As a result of keeping the animals out, there were now a number of small plants growing in the shelter of the house that had been struck from cuttings given to her by women who attended church.

While these plants were mainly hardy native shrubs, Martha was aware that she would be entirely reliant on the dishwater and water she saved from the laundry to keep them alive during the long summer months. In time she was determined to plant shade trees to reduce the effect of the sun on the roof and walls of the house.

She looked with pride at the native Geraldton Wax she had so laboriously tended and which now flourished. When in bloom their massed pink edged white flowers would provide a contrast to the rich blue, white and red Lantana and the mounds of light green daisy bushes with their display of blue centred white flowers. These she thought would be backed by the dark green of Jade and the tall red and white Oleanders that she had planted inside the fence. I really must see if that woman who lives near the church in York will let me take a cutting of that wonderful purple Bougainvillaea some time, she mused. I could then train it along the fence, perhaps over there in the corner.

She looked to the south where the track wound up from the river crossing. Nothing moved and she returned to her sewing and her thoughts.

Robert was quite hopeless when it came to working out the practicalities of living at Bolumbygine. While she loved him dearly, their relationship had rapidly undergone a transformation, so that now she viewed him more as a mother may regard a small child than as a husband on whom she could rely.

She had been trying to devise a means whereby the water she emptied out from the tin tub that served as her bath could be saved for use on the shrubs she had planted. Robert continued to use the shower he had made by piercing holes in the bottom of a four-gallon kerosene tin and hanging it in the shed.

Water governed her life and it had only been when she had threatened to ask Ted Robinson to build her a rainwater tank that Robert had arranged for the plumber at York to erect a two thousand-gallon tank to collect the rainwater off the roof.

Looking up, she caught sight of the tall figure of Dora Sievright making her way up the track through the trees by the church. She really didn't know what she would have done without Dora. Ted Robinson was good hearted and helpful to Robert with church affairs, but his wife Edith had a malicious tongue and was a confirmed gossip. Though she constantly stated her desire for others to call a spade a spade, she forever took offence at the most innocent comment. Martha smiled. At least she had had the best of Edith the only occasion the latter had criticised her to her face. Now that she had Edith's measure, she would never be concerned about her criticism again.

Heaving her swollen body out of the rocking chair, Martha paused to straighten her back prior to making her way through the house to the kitchen to lay the table and make some tea. No sooner had she done so than she heard Dora's firm step on the wooden boards of the back verandah.

Martha raised her voice: "Come in Dora," she said.

Moving to the end of the table she remained standing, leaning forward with her hands on the table as her friend and neighbour came to the screen door. Dora entered carrying a cane basket.

Martha smiled at her and indicating a chair at the side of the table, said: "It's good to see you, Dora, you're just in time to join me for a cup of tea."

The older woman removed the straw hat that had been protecting her face from the September sun, revealing brown hair flecked with grey surrounding a pleasant lined face from which dark eyes kindly surveyed her young friend.

"You look tired, Martha," she said. "I hope you will be sensible now and let the rector take you in to York to have your baby. It is not too late to arrange that, you know."

"The baby's not due for another fortnight, Dora. I'll speak to Robert this evening. He has the bishop coming to Pinjarra and they are going around the churches at the southern end of the parish together, before the bishop goes on to Albany."

"My dear, surely he is not going to be away this close to your time?" Dora was aghast at Robert's proposed absence.

"Robert says that the clergy are so short in number that it's his duty to go about all he can. He has assured me that he will be back in good time before the baby comes." Martha smiled at her unconcernedly and poured the tea.

Dora had been gone some time and the sun had dropped over the western horizon when Martha heard the jingle of harness and the snort of a horse as the buggy came out of the trees below.

She left her place on the verandah and walked heavily towards the shed to meet her husband as the horses came to a stop. He looked at her with tired eyes without comment and, climbing stiffly down, commenced taking the horses out of the small four-wheeled vehicle.

"How are you, Robert?" she asked quietly.

He didn't answer but went on unbuckling the harness. She didn't pursue the subject, knowing that when he was tired he found it an immense effort to carry on a conversation. Reaching into the rear of the buggy she picked up the small tucker box in which he kept the food on his trips and carried it back to the house, where she busied herself with the evening meal.

She heard the dull clang of the tin buckets against the feed bins as Robert put out chaff and oats for the horses in the small yard behind the shed, then the scuffle of their hooves as he let them go into the paddock to find water and feed.

His footsteps sounded on the verandah, and there were small noises as he took the tin bowl to the water tank to wash. At last he came through the door and carried the small communion case into the spare bedroom. She heard him gasp.

"What on earth are you doing to my office, Martha?" he asked as he came to the door of the kitchen.

"Making it into a nursery." She turned to him from the stove.

"That's my office! It's the only place I can write in peace." He sounded petulant as he moved to the table and sat down.

"Robert, you wanted a child and it's nearly here. We have to have a nursery and, in any case, you're rarely home." She ladled the soup into a deep dish and placed it in front of him, "Now, eat up this soup. There's plenty and I have some mutton casserole to follow."

He looked at her with deep-set brooding eyes and then, dropping them, said grace silently. Reaching across the table he took a piece of bread and picking up a spoon began to eat.

Martha continued to stand at the stove and watch her husband as, without a word, he ate his evening meal.

The next morning, while they sat at their breakfast, Martha raised the matter of the coming birth of their child.

"What do you mean, you think you should go into York to await the arrival of the baby!" he exclaimed in exasperated tones. "The baby is not due until the first week in October and it is only the sixteenth of September now."

"I thought you would be less concerned about me if I was in town," Martha said quietly, sitting very straight on her chair. "You would be better able to give your full attention to the bishop next week if I was in York under the eyes of Doctor Ewell."

He sat back in his chair and looked at her with his deep-set eyes. "I don't know what gets into you sometimes, Martha. You know we can't afford for you to board in York for three weeks and we could hardly accept charity."

"Robert," she persisted, "it wouldn't be accepting charity to accept Mrs Ewell's kind invitation to go in and stay with her. After all, I had Mrs Ewell's two children to stay here for a week during May while she was helping Dr Ewell with that epidemic of influenza amongst the timber workers at the West Dale sawmill."

"Mrs Ewell may be a trained nurse but she would have been far better employed looking after her children than trying to be Florence Nightingale to those men at the mill. I don't approve of one woman being with fifty men in those rough huts."

"Robert, her husband was there!"

Robert stood up from the table and pushed his chair in.

"I don't care who was there," he said savagely, "her place was with the children, not gadding about all over the district. It is my wish that you stay here until the baby is due and then I'll take you to the hospital in York."

With that he turned away and swung out of the house and across to the shed.

Martha stood clutching the end of the table, a tear running down her cheek. I'll never be able to change him, she thought, he is so stubborn. Doesn't he realise that babies don't suit their arrival to the visits of bishops?

Ten days later on the twenty seventh of September 1893, while Robert Gladwell was accompanying the bishop through the southern part of the wide area he covered, Martha gave birth to their first child in the lonely rectory at Bolumbygine aided only by Dora Sievright.

The little baby boy thrived from the start and his mother,

disdaining the advice of both Mrs Sievright and Mrs Robinson, was up and about the next day. By the time her husband arrived home three days late, to learn of the arrival of his son and heir, she had already driven in with the Robinsons in their sulky to the Beverley doctor and registered the child's birth at the Court House.

Robert gave no indication that he was in anyway put out by the baby not waiting for his return before making his entry into the world. He was pleased to find that his wife had named the child George, after his father, though less gratified to be informed that his wife had also given him her family name Hayward.

By the time he returned from yet another tour of his far flung parish and had christened his son with due ceremony in the church, Martha was again pregnant.

So their life progressed. Robert was forever away for periods of up to a month at a time, driving around his far-flung parish, visiting isolated farms and conducting services in the other churches, returning to the small stone house on the hill at Bolumbygine between times to take services there.

Rarely a twelve-month passed without a new baby being born to them. Though Robert had reluctantly agreed to Dora Sievright's earnest entreaty that Martha should have the others in the York Hospital under the care of the kindly doctor there, Martha was never away for more than a week after the event.

****

CHAPTER 6
February 1902

Having persuaded Robert to let her have her own horse and sulky, Martha was alone when she arrived at Dora's garden gate to collect her brood of children after the birth of her sixth child, Timothy Hayward Gladwell.

"Mummy, Mummy, have you brought the new baby with you?" Anthony Hayward Gladwell propelled himself around the corner of the Sievright's house and stopped briefly to pick the three-pronged burr of a doublegee from his bare foot.

"Yes, of course I have dear," said his mother, as she climbed stiffly down and ruffled the dark curls of her five-year-old son as he threw himself upon her.

Martha looked up and saw that her eldest son George, ever sensible, had gone to the head of the skewbald mare that stood flecked with sweat after drawing the sulky through the soft sand of the river crossing.

Martha called: "Thank you George. Fairy's tired. It was a hot drive today."

She reached under the seat of the sulky and pulled out a large wickerwork baby basket, which she picked up in her arms then, turning, saw Dora Sievright coming towards her. The Gladwell children followed. Elizabeth aged seven, neat and clean as always with her hair freshly brushed, was holding her equally immaculate younger sister Rebecca by the hand as the tot marched solemnly along, a thumb firmly in place in her mouth. Behind them Douglas, aged six, appeared around the corner of the bathroom that projected off the verandah and, with a wild yell, charged across the dusty space towards the back gate.

Reaching it at the same moment as his sisters, he pushed his way through and received a jab from a sharp elbow in his stomach as he did so.

He gasped and jerked forward momentarily then, drawing himself upright, he clenched his fist and raised it threateningly to his elder sister. "You do that again and I'll belt you one," he shouted, scowling at her horribly.

"Douglas!" admonished his mother, "behave yourself."

Douglas took one look at his mother's stern face and decided to defer retribution.

His mother could see the sweet innocent expression on her elder daughter's face and felt her mouth twitch. She had no doubt that Elizabeth would be well able to take care of herself when faced with the worst that Douglas could do.

She looked towards her friend. "Dora, I am so glad to come home! I do nothing but worry all the time I am away from them. I hope they were no trouble."

Dora had scooped up Rebecca and had the child sitting on her hip. "My dear, they really are little trouble," she replied placidly with a smile. "George has been a great help to Fred around the farm and Elizabeth has looked after Rebecca beautifully. As long as we keep Anthony and Douglas well supplied with food they amuse themselves. Now bring the little one in and you can bath him while I get the tea."

She peered into the basket and twitched the light cotton blanket back from the baby's face with her free hand.

"Another one from the same mould, I see," she said, looking at the crinkled red face and shock of black hair, then stood back to let the children who were crowding around her see into the bassinet.

Martha showed the children their new brother Timothy, then carried the baby in his basket into the Sievright's house while George led the mare away with the sulky and tethered her in the shade of the pepper tree that overhung the garden fence.

Martha bathed the baby while Dora, with Elizabeth's help,

laid the table for tea. He was comfortably back in his basket on the floor when Dora sent Anthony out to ring the bell for the men to come up from the sheds for their afternoon tea.

Martha was seated with Dora at the table and the Gladwell children perched in a line along the edge of the verandah drinking lemonade and eating bread and jam when Fred Sievright marched up to the house followed by his two boys, Young Fred and Peter.

Young Fred grinned at the row of sticky fingered children. He stubbed his cigarette out before stepping onto the verandah for his mother did not approve of smoking in the house, even though a young man of twenty could mostly please himself what he did. Rubbing his feet on the old wheat bag that served as a mat at the back door, he entered the kitchen.

His brother Peter, four years his junior, but taller, and in the Gladwell children's eyes just as daunting, caught sight of Elizabeth's serious face and winked at her, then called to George. "You'll be glad to have your mother back now. You won't have so much work to do at the rectory as you have here."

George grinned. Peter was his special friend and he knew that Peter was well aware just how much work he did do at home, where he was responsible for feeding not only the horses and grooming them, but the pigs and chickens too. Sometimes though, Elizabeth would help out with the chooks when he had too much homework to do after a long day at school.

"Hello Martha!" said Fred as he peered into the bassinet at the baby. "He's a proper chip off the old block, isn't he?" He turned away and, drawing a chair up to the table, sat down and reached for the plate of bread and butter and passed it to his guest.

"Where's the reverend? Is he still down at Williams? I don't know how you put up with his gallivanting around the parish like he does." He spread jam on his bread and taking a mouthful, sat back.

Martha said nothing, but took a sip from her cup.

Dora intervened sharply. "Fred, don't you tease. You know

that Robert Gladwell is the hardest working clergyman we've ever had in these parts and, from what I hear, people really appreciate the way he visits even the loneliest farms out in the bush and the miners at Southern Cross. When we were over to Gilgering last New Year, I heard one woman say that it was not too much for her to walk the four miles to church to hear Mr Gladwell preach when he could take the trouble to come out to her family on the farm as often as he does."

"Don't go on, Dora," Fred said. "Martha knows that I think a great deal of Robert as a churchman. It's just that I think he could have been here at this time to help her when she is first home with a new baby. I warrant he hasn't seen this new arrival even though he could have caught the train up from Pingelly or Narrogin when he was there this week."

Martha looked up. "To tell you the truth," she responded spiritedly, "he would have thought that a luxury we could ill afford and in any case he has little time when he is on the circuit around the southern end of the parish. We manage very well these days, now that George has grown big enough to help with the animals and Elizabeth is so good with Rebecca."

Dora caught her husband's eye and shook her head slightly, then changed the subject. "I don't want to hurry you away Martha, but it's after four o'clock and we have to load the sulky with the children's things. I've cooked a leg of mutton, so that you'll have that for tomorrow and I baked two loaves for you this morning."

The three Gladwell children met outside the gates of the Beverley schoolyard as usual after school. Elizabeth carried the small wooden case in which she brought her sandwiches every day.

Douglas waved his hands and danced about with excitement as he sought to persuade his elder brother to go down the main street to where the track of the Great Southern

Railway from Albany crossed over the road and entered the station.

"George," he cried, " I want to go and see the new flyer that is coming up from Perth today. It's a very special engine."

"You know we can't George," his sister said. "Mother, says we are always to go straight home as otherwise Douglas gets too tired and then he wheezes."

George looked indecisively at his sister. He too had heard of the expected arrival in the town of the new locomotive. "I don't think it's coming until quite late, Douglas, and we can't wait until dark."

"We certainly couldn't," added Elizabeth. "If we aren't home on time, Mother will be worried and that isn't fair when father is away and she has the others to look after."

Douglas ran off towards the railway station shouting "I don't care what Elizabeth says, I want to see the train. The other kids are allowed to go and see it. I will too."

George ran after him, the smaller boy keeping ahead of him as he ran past the Post Office. Dodging people standing outside the store, Douglas ran on and looking back at his brother, stumbled, sprawling on the track in front of a locomotive that was leaving the station's only platform.

George stopped and threw his hands up. Behind him Elizabeth screamed and, dropping her school box, ran wildly for the crumpled figure on the line. Panting, she grasped Douglas's outstretched hand and tried to pull him from between the rails as she felt rather than saw the engine grind closer, its brakes squealing.

George watched in horror, his feet rooted to the ground as the slight figure pulled in vain at the little boy. His mouth opened and the rising scream was caught in his mouth as amid the cries of the adults behind him, a tall figure raced past. Flinging Elizabeth to one side the man bent to scoop up Douglas in mid stride, just as the train reached the place where the child had been, then passed on until, brakes squealing, it shuddered to a stop in the middle of the street. George gulped as a wave of nausea engulfed him and he vomited into the gutter.

Gentle hands picked Elizabeth up from the gravel beside the track and dusted her down.

"Now me darlin', let's look at yer," said a voice with a lilting brogue.

She looked up into a pair of brown eyes that were smiling at her from a red face, and said nothing.

The man with the red face produced a large white handkerchief and holding it towards her, he said. "Spit on it and oi'l wipe some o'the dust off that graze on yer cheek. Good, that's a fine lass."

Elizabeth felt the damp cloth on her face, which she now realised was stinging. "Thank you, sir," she said, politely. Then, remembering that she hadn't seen Douglas, she looked for him over the big man's shoulder as he crouched before her. He stood up and she could see that he was wearing the round white collar of a priest.

"Are they all right, Father?" A small man in blue overalls asked, as he crunched towards them from the locomotive. "I couldn't stop her in time. That little kid gave me no chance."

"Don't you worry, I saw what happened. The little devil just ran straight in front of the train. He was lucky that this young fellah was so quick, as no matter how much pluck the little girl had, she couldn't have moved him off the rail before the engine hit him."

"I would never have been able to grab him so easily if she hadn't had his hand. She was a game little thing, never stopped to look at the loco, just tried to get him off the track." The tall man with the yellow hair smiled down at her.

Elizabeth felt warmth spread all over her as his eyes surveyed her and she straightened her dress and felt to make sure that her ribbon was still in her hair. Looking away she saw that the priest was regarding her quizzically. Confused, she dropped her eyes to her feet.

"That's Mr Gladwell's little girl, from out at Bolumbygine," said another voice, "and there is her little brother and the elder boy too. Young George isn't it?"

"Well now, I've to got to go home to York. I can go around that way and drop them home," the priest said. He turned to the man with the yellow hair. "What's your name? I'm Father O'Mear and I'd like to shake your hand, after what you did."

"Bill Pederick, Father," he put out his hand and returned the priest's handclasp. "I'm on my way to Spencers Brook. I've been over to Adelaide to see my folks and going back to the Goldfields," he added.

"Well, if you need a reference or a feed sometime and you're in York, oi'll be only too pleased to see you." The priest smiled at the younger man. "Now oi'll just gather up my passengers and we can get going. We don't want their mother coming in to look for them do we?"

Father O'Mear let his horse and sulky down into the river crossing at Bolumbygine and, as the wheels lurched through the deep sand of the dry watercourse, he stole a look at the little figure sitting upright on the seat beside him.

Hmm, he mused; this one is a quiet child, very well brought up though, and polite.

The two boys sitting on the tray behind the bench seat had been quite talkative once they had got over their initial shyness. There wasn't much that the catholic priest didn't know about the Gladwell family by now, as with consummate skill he had drawn the boys out. An intelligent pair of boys, especially the little tacker, he was already well over his scare and positively leaping out of his skin with nervous energy. However, it was their sister that intrigued him. She was as quick as a whip, but quiet and reserved. She had considered everything he said carefully before responding, and when she did some of her answers had surprised him, coming as they did from such a young child.

The horse pulled up the steep rise out of the river and along the bank before turning off to the small stone house on the hill that was the children's home.

As they drew up at the garden gate a young woman came onto the verandah, an infant in her arms. Two more children came around the side of the house and stopped short to stare at the stranger.

She's a pretty lass and must find it difficult this far from town when her husband is off around his parish, he thought. He knew of Robert Gladwell and was aware that he constantly travelled in his efforts to cover the area for which he was responsible.

"Oi'm, Patrick O'Mear," he said. "Oi've just given your charming children a lift out from town as oi'm on me way through here to see some of me flock a bit further down the valley before going to York."

Martha had walked out to the sulky as he said this. She looked up at him as he sat on the seat holding the horses while letting the boys get down from the back. Elizabeth continued to sit straight primly beside him, holding her luncheon box on her knees.

"Thank you Father, for bringing them with you. Though I have taught them always to refuse a lift from strangers. I hope it was not too much out of your way." Martha's keen eyes had noted that Elizabeth had a bad graze on her cheek and that her smock dress, usually so clean, was showing evidence of a fall. There was also a small tear in Douglas's trousers. That was not so unusual.

George came up to her and said earnestly. "Douglas had an accident, mama. He fell in front of the railway train and Elizabeth tried to pull him out of the way."

"A big man with yellow hair knocked her over and picked me up. We were quite all right," added Douglas excitedly.

Martha put her hand to her mouth and cast an enquiring glance at the priest.

"It's all right, Mrs Gladwell, they are quite unharmed. This little lady was the heroine of the hour and though the little chap had a fright, as you can see he is undisturbed by his experience. A young man from South Australia, who gave me his name as Bill Pederick, reached them first. It was he who whisked them both out of the way of the locomotive in good time and there was no harm done, so don't you fret."

Martha continued to look into the smiling eyes of the priest and, reassured by what she saw there, hitched the child on her hip and turned to the two boys.

"Boys, you get off and wash now." Turning back to her daughter, she said quietly. "Thank you Elizabeth, I know you always try to take care of the little ones and I am very proud of what you have done today."

Father O'Mear turned to the small girl sitting so quietly beside him and smiled. Gathering the reins in his left hand he reached out to her with his right and when she had put her small hand in his, he shook it gravely.

"You had better get down now and go to your mother. She'll be wanting your help soon to set the table for your tea."

"Oh," said Martha in confusion. "Will you come in please and have a cup of tea with us now? I am sorry, I quite forgot and don't know what you must think of me."

O'Mear shook his head. "No thank you, I have to move on. I've still a fair way to go before I reach York, as you would well know. If I may I will call in one day when I am passing and perhaps I'll meet your husband. I have heard a lot about him and would like to have the opportunity of making his acquaintance. Good day to you Ma'am, and to you Miss Elizabeth." He raised his hat and with a click of his tongue drove his horse around in a circle and back to where the track went on down the valley to Broughton Park and York.

****

CHAPTER 7
November 1902

With the approach of Christmas, Martha was not surprised when Edith Robinson, returning from a trip into Beverley, brought her a letter from her mother in England.

Edith had little tact and having already accepted Martha's invitation to join her and Robert for a cup of tea, suggested that she make the tea while Martha read her mother's letter to Robert at the kitchen table.

Martha sensed quite correctly that the older woman was consumed by curiosity as to the contents of the letter and having no desire to provide ammunition for Edith's tittle tattle she laid the letter aside on the kitchen dresser. She knocked on the door of the nursery and opening it told her husband, who was writing at his desk in the corner of the room, that tea would be ready in a few minutes.

"I should be getting home and leave you and the Rector to enjoy your tea in peace," Edith said with a sniff.

"Please yourself Edith," Martha said, with a slight shrug of her shoulders. "I invited you to have tea because I was grateful to you for picking up our mail and I enjoy your company. You haven't been here for some time and it would be nice to have you for tea while Robert is home."

Edith took a deep breath and her opportunity. "Well, you know I would come to see you more often, Martha," she boomed in her deep voice, "but Dora Sievright is often here and she was so rude to me that I have decided never speak to her again."

Martha looked at her pityingly. "I am sorry you feel like that Edith, as I believe you could be missing some interesting afternoons, particularly when young Mrs Webb comes over here from Broughton. She is such a polished woman and keeps in close touch with what is going on in Perth and the outside world."

Edith sat down with a bang. "Young Mrs Webb!" she exclaimed. "I didn't know that she came calling, here at the rectory. I thought she spent all her time at their town house down at Guildford. Why has she been spending more time up here? I always understood she preferred city life. Perhaps the bad seasons and the poor prices for wool have left even the Webbs short of money?"

"I don't know," said Martha shortly. "She has been dropping over here quite regularly in that smart little surrey of hers on a Thursday, which is the day Dora comes here too. I'd be delighted if you would care to join us next week, Edith."

Warring emotions chased each other over Edith's face as she pondered this information. "I am not sure what I have on next week, Martha," she said, to Martha's inward amusement. "I'll let you know tomorrow if I can fit it in."

"Fit in what Mrs Robinson?" Robert asked, as he came into the kitchen.

Passing the dresser he saw the letter from Martha's mother and taking it up peered short-sightedly at the postmark. "Ah, ha!" he cried, "A letter from home, and your mother's handwriting. Have you read it?"

"Not yet, I haven't opened it."

"Ah, so I see," he laid the letter on the table beside Martha and turning to his guest asked, "Well, Mrs Robinson, and how are the boys?"

Edith sensed an opportunity to unburden herself to a sympathetic ear and started to relate the latest difficulties she was having with her children.

Martha poured the tea and passed around some oatcakes then, bored with the conversation, slit open the envelope before her and started to read its contents. After reading the first few lines she stopped and went back to the beginning, her face turning white. As she read, the colour came back into her cheeks.

Robert, listening with apparent interest to Edith's litany of complaint, cocked an enquiring eyebrow at his wife, only to be ignored. Having read the letter for a third time Martha quietly put it to one side and rejoined the conversation.

After Edith had finally taken herself off down the hill, Robert came back to the kitchen.

"What did your mother have to say, Martha?"

"I was so upset that I almost blurted out her news in front of Edith Robinson."

"And?" prompted Robert, gently.

"Grandfather Jones has died. I am so sorry I'll never see him again, I always loved him so much and mother will miss him too."

"May I read her letter, Martha?"

"Please do. I'll clear the table, and get on with the evening meal." She looked at the clock on the mantelpiece. "Four o'clock, the children will be home shortly."

Robert sat at the table to read the letter then looked up. "Did you realise that your grandfather had left you some money?"

"Did he? I was more concerned with his death and the effect that would have on mother."

"Well, he did. Your mother says here that his partner is arranging to send it out to you. That was very good of him," he added.

Martha turned around from the stove and stood looking at him as he sat tipping the chair back, one leg thrust out before him as he read the letter again.

"Hmm, your mother doesn't say how much money is involved. I wonder if there would be enough for a nice window for the church. In his memory, of course."

Martha put her hands on her hips, two red spots appearing on her cheeks. "I don't know what gets into you sometimes, Robert. I don't care how much money Grandfather has left to me. I wish he hadn't died and was still alive to support mother when father is being difficult. If there is any money, it certainly won't be going towards a window for the church. It will be going to build a bathroom onto this house."

"But what is the point of that, Martha? We've managed very well without one for the last ten years and in any case the rectory belongs to the church. The church owns the land and provided most of the money for me to build the house here. There is no sense in putting any more of our own money into this property when we don't own it. Anyway we may be asked to move to another parish before long. Now that more ordained priests are arriving in the state they will need to alter the parish boundaries so that each is centred on a township like Beverley."

"Well, Robert, just you make sure of one thing. I must have a bathroom and I'll either have one here or at the next place we live. I am not bathing in a tin tub for the rest of my life!"

Two months after this conversation, Martha received a polite letter from the manager of the West Australian Bank in York advising her that a sum of money had been transferred from England and was being held by the bank pending her instructions.

Robert was at home and immediately agreed to drive her into York the next day.

The next morning, after the children had gone off to school in Beverley, Martha took the younger children down to Dora to leave them with her while they were in York.

Setting out in the buggy they crossed the ridge behind the rectory and drove along the unmade track through gum trees standing in all the glory of fresh new bark. The salmon gums were at their best, the layer of pink bark gleaming on their limbs while on the ground below lay the twisted debris of the previous year. Reaching level ground by the river, the horses broke into a trot as they followed the watercourse. They crossed over the bridge and passed the Broughton Park homestead, its spacious two storied house sitting graciously amongst white gums against a granite hill. Following the track as it wound through the trees they came at last to the Avon River and followed it downstream to York.

Robert drove the buggy into the town and tied the horses to the rail outside the bank, before handing Martha down into the dusty street. They entered the small building but were disappointed to learn from a clerk that the manager was out of town until midday. They made an appointment to see him on his return.

As they left the bank Martha caught sight of Father O'Mear, who immediately came across the street to greet them. Under the friendly influence of the catholic priest Robert rapidly surrendered his habitual reserve and was soon so deep in animated conversation that when Martha excused herself to go along the street to the drapery store, he barely acknowledged her departure.

Martha walked down the sidewalk with a light heart, telling herself it was a pity they didn't see more people like Father O'Mear, with whom Robert could engage in stimulating discussion. She smiled as she turned into the shop; he certainly seemed to be enjoying himself.

Sorting through some cotton voile that the saleswoman had laid out on the counter for her inspection she was suddenly aware of galloping hooves outside the shop as a pair of horses bolted past with a light buggy. Immediately all the people in the shop ran out to see what was going on.

Further down the street Patrick O'Mear's keen ears had caught the buzz of excitement and he looked up. Hearing flying hooves he turned, to see over the heads of the people outside the Post Office a light four wheeled surrey racing towards him, a young woman leaning back on the reins trying to stop the bolting horses.

"We've got to stop this, Gladwell," he cried, interrupting

Robert's argument and pointing to indicate the source of his concern. He ran into the middle of the road with Robert close behind him.

"Wait 'till they come up to us and then you grab the off side animal's head while I do the same for the other."

Robert felt no fear, just a queer sort of elation to be joining with O'Mear in this mad enterprise and, seeing the big Irishman launch himself at one horse, he sprang at the other. The animals swerved away from the two men and, colliding, checked momentarily, by which time their bits had been grasped tightly and heavy weights were hanging on their straining heads.

Robert, his right arm outstretched, had grasped the bit a fraction of a moment before the animal's shoulder had cannoned into him, sweeping his feet off the ground. Much to his surprise he found his left hand was entwined in the animal's mane and he hung on for dear life, while the frightened horses swerved, then propped and almost came down as the weight of the surrey drove the pole up high between them.

They all came to a sliding stop and Robert found himself holding both animals heads as, eyes starting, they stood with ears back and chests heaving.

Looking between the horses he saw the driver, a fine looking woman with flame red hair glaring at him as, with both hands holding the reins, she leaned back against the perch seat, one foot braced against the dashboard. Two boys, aged perhaps ten or twelve years, stood on the tray behind and clung to the back of the driver's seat.

Father O'Mear, very much the worse for wear, limped up to him, his hat battered and crammed on the side of his head. Putting one hand on the nearside horse he passed Robert his own dust covered hat with the other.

"Well done Gladwell!" he exclaimed, his eyes dancing. His big face split into a wide grin. "Here's yer hat. Oi lost me grip and got bowled head over heels, but you stuck with them like a terrier, boyo." He thumped Robert on the back with a great paw.

"If you two schoolboys would stop congratulating yourselves and will listen to me, I could get down to see if the horses have come to harm," said the redhead.

O'Mear stiffened and he squinted over the horses' backs into a pair of green eyes.

"Begorra," he said, "and isn't it grateful you should be, the Reverend Mr Gladwell and oi having come to your rescue. Would you have Irish blood in yer, Mrs Webb? For faith it's only the Irish are as ungrateful when the Lord has provided his instruments to save them. If it wasn't for Mr Gladwell here, you and your two sons would be strawberry jam under this tiddy little wagon at the end of the street. Hold these horses Gladwell and I'll help the lady to the ground so that she can the better recover her breath."

Indeed the lady was in a towering rage and nothing that O'Mear had said had done anything to assuage this.

"You big log, it was a damn fool dog barking that caused them to bolt. They wouldn't have got away from me. If I had been able to run them out of town and down the road a stretch, they would have tired themselves out and would have calmed down." She looked down at O'Mear standing quietly beside the surrey, then blushed to the roots of her hair. "Oh, I'm sorry, I really am most grateful to you both, but it infuriates me when men don't believe that women can deal with an emergency."

O'Mear grinned and, reaching up, he swung her down to the ground.

"My, you're a big man Father, you're wasted in the church," she said, glancing up at him with a twinkle in her green eyes, then bent to dust her skirt down.

O'Mear ignored her and told the two boys to climb down.

Charlotte Webb looked up as Martha reached Robert.

"Oh, hello Martha. I have never met your husband before.

He and Father O'Mear here have just saved my life, or so they would have me believe, not giving women any credit for sense or ability to handle a pair of spirited hacks. I am grateful just the same, even if I don't appear to be, as the boys were getting worried." She looked down at Robert's legs and raised her hands to her face in horror. "Oh, Mr Gladwell, I am sorry, you've torn your trousers and your leg is bleeding while I'm blathering on."

She stepped forward and, raising the grey serge of his trouser cuff, inspected the damage. She showed it to Martha who could see that the material was indeed torn and beneath it Robert's skin had been torn from the shin in a long shallow wound, the skin still attached at the bottom like a curled wood shaving taken by a carpenter's plane.

Robert grinned at O'Mear. "It's nothing," he said casually, enjoying the attention of the two women. "The sharp edge of a hoof probably caught my leg. It'll soon heal with a drop of Stockholm Tar. My foot is more painful where I think the horse stood on me."

Charlotte ignored him. "Martha, you had better take him straight up to Doctor Ewell and get him to look at this. I am really sorry that he has been hurt, please forgive me." Charlotte looked almost contrite as she turned her head and looked up at Robert.

Martha told her not to worry and calling one of the bystanders to hold the horses, said goodbye to Charlotte and O'Mear. She shepherded Robert to their buggy and sat him down while she inspected his leg, then drove him across the river by the town bridge to the doctor's house.

Here they had to wait an hour until the doctor returned from a visit and washed and dressed not only Robert's shin but also the deep cut in the top of his foot.

As a result they forgot their appointment with the bank manager and didn't get back to Bolumbygine until dusk.

****

CHAPTER 8

It only takes a speck of dirt

The next morning Robert's leg and foot were sore and once the children had gone to school Martha bathed his wounds with warm salt water and applied the iodine that Dr Ewell had given her. The pain easing, Robert moved to the verandah and sat in the rocking chair with his foot on an old kerosene box that Martha had covered with cloth as a stool.

After several days of rest the wound in Robert's foot began to heal and he decided that he was well enough to make the trip to York to complete their business with the bank.

On the way into town, Robert complained of a general nausea and feverishness. Laying her hand on his forehead Martha found him cold and clammy. Concerned, she insisted they go to the doctor before seeing the bank manager.

They found Dr Ewell at the hospital and, having examined Robert, who by this time was having difficulty in opening his mouth, the doctor ordered a room to be prepared for him. Once he was in bed and the curtains drawn against the strong sunlight the doctor returned and, having made sure his patient was comfortable, called Martha and the matron to his office at the end of the building.

"Mrs Gladwell," he said. "We'll have to keep your husband here for a few days. I am not sure of the cause of his condition, though it may be an infection has entered his body through his wounds. The stiffness in his neck and jaw concerns me and it could be evidence that the bacillus is attacking the central nervous system. The best way to deal with that is to keep him quiet in a darkened room with plenty of nourishing fluids."

Martha, her eyes even bigger than normal, regarded him worriedly. "What exactly do you think he has picked up, Doctor?" She asked.

"I don't know precisely. At least we'll be able to keep him quiet here."

He smiled at her. What a pretty little thing she is, he thought. You would never believe that she has that tribe of children out there. The trouble with these Bible bashers is so often that they are not practical people and leave their womenfolk to cope not only with the children, but everything else around the home.

He became aware that Martha was speaking. "What was that you said, my dear?" he asked.

Martha repeated her question.

"Yes, I do think that you should come into town for a few days to be with him. Have you any friends or neighbours who could look after the children? If you can arrange that, I think it would be as well if you stayed here at the hospital." He turned to the matron. "Have you a room that Mrs Gladwell could use for a few days, until her husband is over the worst of this?"

The matron hesitated, then smiled. "Why certainly, we have a spare room in the nursing quarters which I am sure Mrs Gladwell would find comfortable."

With everything arranged for her stay in York, Martha drove out to Bolumbygine to see her neighbours. Dora Sievright was more than willing to look after the little ones with Elizabeth's help, and Edith Robinson, once she realised how serious Robert's illness was, unhesitatingly agreed to take George, Douglas and Anthony.

Martha returned to York the next morning and, having left her mare in the paddock behind the Residency, carried her valise to the staff quarters next door.

When the matron saw her coming across the yard towards the verandah of the hospital she beckoned her urgently, with her finger to her lips.

"Come into my office my dear and I'll bring you up to date with his condition."

Martha sat uncomfortably on a hard chair just inside the

door while the matron lowered her large body behind her desk, then swung around towards her and spoke in a quiet voice.

"Doctor has asked me to tell you that he has confirmed his diagnosis and we are going to be in for a long row."

Martha clasped her hands together and leaned forward. "Matron, what is wrong?"

"It's quite nasty. He appears to have picked up tetanus from the dust of the road when either his leg or foot was cut. The infection is closely associated with grazing animals and lives in their stomach, reaching the earth in their droppings. It is very easy for the bacillus to enter the body when a wound is contaminated with dirt from a road where animals are regularly passing to and fro."

"Yes, I can understand that, but what can be done for Robert?"

"We have to keep him quiet and try to minimise the occurrence of spasm. The infection is following the classic course and he had a difficult night as the stiffness in his neck and jaw spread to the muscles of his trunk and limbs. You must be prepared for him to appear distressed sometimes, especially when he is suffering a spasm. The doctor has him under sedation, but we have to be careful not to touch him with cold hands or to stimulate him to sudden movement as he may go into severe muscular contractions."

"Matron, isn't tetanus often fatal?" Martha enquired anxiously.

"Yes it is, if the patient is not nursed carefully, but you brought him in as soon as the symptoms became apparent and we have been able to keep him quiet so far. Doctor feels we have every chance of bringing him through this. He is arranging for notices to be put up in the town to ask everyone to keep noise to a minimum. However, come and see him. Sister Malloy is sitting with him just now."

Martha followed the matron to the room at the far end of the verandah. Robert looked terrible, his face almost blue as he lay exhausted on the bed. Malloy signalled them urgently to go outside, where she joined them.

"He had a bad turn just now, Matron," she whispered, "I think we should send for the Doctor."

"This is Mrs Gladwell, Sister," whispered the matron, looking at her meaningfully. "She has come to stay with us until Mr Gladwell is out of danger." She turned to Martha. "Sister Malloy has had a great deal of experience, Mrs Gladwell, and she will explain to you how to cope if he should have a spasm when you are with him. I think we should go back to my office and leave her to care for her patient just now."

Robert's condition was critical all that day and the following night. The hospital's trained staff constantly attended him. Martha was not allowed to be alone with him as the spasms were harrowing in the extreme. Not only did they cause his body to arch in pain so that he was resting on his head and his heels, but the effect on his chest muscles was such that it was only with the greatest difficulty that he could breathe.

By Saturday it was apparent to them all that his condition was very serious and Doctor Ewell had had to employ drastic measures, including the use of chloroform when the spasms of contraction were most severe and frequent. The nurses were tired out and Martha had been accepted by the matron as capable of taking her turn in nursing him.

It was after nine o'clock in the evening and Martha was handing over to Sister Malloy when there was a disturbance at the front of the building.

Hearing drunken voices and heavy footfalls coming along the verandah they looked at each other in horror. Martha flew out of the room and ran towards the source of the noise, closely followed by Malloy.

Two men were weaving their way towards her, their arms around each other, one streaming blood from a cut over his eye.

"Well, and what have we here, Arthur me boy?" The speaker, the younger of the two, a big blonde haired man, his face flushed with alcohol, swayed slightly. "Here's a nice little bit of goods," he said, leering at Martha. "Didn't know there was anyone like her in this godforsaken place. We only see the leathery faced lot around here; must be one that the bosses keep for themselves," he added drunkenly in a clearly audible aside.

A cry came from the sick man's room and Malloy, turning on her heel, hurried off.

Martha pulled herself up to her full height and looked them both in the eye. "There is a very sick man in a room at the far end of the verandah," she said tersely, "and we must ask you to be quiet until one of the sisters can attend to you."

The blonde man laughed. "Sure, delighted to do whatever you like. Why don't you and me just slip into one of these rooms here and have a little drink. Then we can get to know one another." He felt in the back pocket of his trousers and with great difficulty extracted a flat half bottle of whisky.

"You put that back in your pocket and bring your friend along, but be quiet." Martha moved to lead them into the treatment room.

The other man stretched out his hand and caught her shoulder. "Now lass, don't go on so. We don't mean any harm, I just need a little tender loving care. Some bastard cut me face with a bottle."

"Don't count on it," she said furiously and shrugged off his hand.

The two men followed her into the room where she made the man with the cut face sit down in a chair while his blonde friend stood propped against the wall. Martha looked at the glass-fronted cupboards and having tried the latches realised that they were locked.

"Sister has the key. I'll have to ask her to come so that we can find something to put on that cut." She picked up a towel from the worktop and passed it to the man on the chair. "Hold this to your eye."

As she made for the door, the blonde man put out his arm to stop her. "Give us a kiss," he leered at her drunkenly.

She stood back and looked at him with disgust. "Get out of my way," she said.

He stood in front of her, rocking onto his toes and grinned in admiration. "Proper little spitfire ain't yer nurse. It'd be great to tame this one, Arthur."

His friend lifted his head. "Leave her alone, Bill, and let her fix this cut."

The big man turned and focusing his eyes with difficulty looked at his friend. "Wha's the matter with yer, Arthur?" he said belligerently. "She'd not be such a bad sort. An' I bet she'd like it. I can always tell. You would, wouldn't you love?" He moved towards Martha who, backing away, looked wildly around her for something to defend herself with. Seeing a heavy enamel pan lying on the worktop beside her, she took the handle in both her hands and brought it down on his head.

There was a deep clang and Arthur winced.

The blonde man's eyes blinked and he shook his head in amazement.

Martha had a moment of fright when she realised that he was still on his feet. She wondered vaguely what he would do next. Not waiting to find out, she raised the pan and hit him again with all her strength. Slowly his legs buckled and like a felled log, he dropped to the floor and lay there unmoving.

Martha regarded him warily, the pan still clasped in her hands. Finally, satisfied there was no further need for it, she laid it to one side. She turned to Arthur, who was regarding her with wide eyes, and reached forward and lifted the towel from the cut over his eye, gravely surveying the damage. Replacing the towel, she took his hand and placed it over it, saying as she did so. "Now you keep that towel pressed firmly over that eye and wait here until I can find someone to attend to that cut. I won't be long."

Stepping around Bill, she marched down the verandah to Robert's room at the far end.

The first thing she saw as she came through the door was

Robert lying with his head arched back on the pillow, the bedclothes thrown aside and Sister Malloy sitting at the bedside holding Robert's hand.

Martha stopped, her hands to her mouth, her eyes staring. "Sister, is he all right?" she whispered. She ran to the side of the bed and looked down at her husband.

"He's not breathing. Why isn't he breathing?" she cried distractedly.

Malloy lifted her head with an effort. "The noise they made set him off into another spasm, and in the middle of it all, he just gave up. I am so sorry, I did what I could, but he gave up." Her face crumpled and she burst into tears.

Martha put her arm around Malloy to console her.

****

Chapter 9

Do we go home or stay here?

Father Patrick O'Mear finished reading the burial service with a prayer. He opened his eyes, paused, and looked across the valley to the distant hills, before nodding to Ted Robinson, who led Martha forward to the graveside where she stood with bowed head.

What a wicked waste of a man, he thought. Gladwell wasn't such a bad lad for an anglican. I wonder what he's thinking of me, of all people, reading the anglican burial service over his body. Not that you have to be ordained to read a burial service. Well, she wanted a priest and there wasn't another available and, as that brave little lass said, we are all one before God. I just hope the powers that be take the same view; not only the anglicans, but our lot too.

He shrugged and looked across the grave to where the two eldest Gladwell children stood with Mrs Sievright in the harsh sunlight. Fine woman that, he thought, hard working and lost what good looks she ever had. This climate soaks up the oils out of the skin, turns it all leathery. Well, not all women suffer that. Mrs Gladwell has a wonderful complexion, as do many of the girls in Ireland.

Here she is now, coming to speak to me, dry eyed too. I would expect her to shed her tears in private. I wonder what will happen to her and the children now. Without doubt they'll go back to the old dart. It'll not be easy for her, a young woman with six children to care for. She can't be more than thirty-one or two. I hope Gladwell's family is well off. They could be. His speech was that of an educated man.

Aloud he addressed Martha. "Thank you for giving me the privilege of taking this service today," he smiled sympathetically.

She came close to the priest and stretching out her hand laid it on his arm. "Thank you Father. Robert would have been pleased with the reading. I wanted him to be buried here at his first church and he always said it should be as soon as possible in this climate."

O'Mear was surprised at her pragmatic approach to life, and looked it.

"You probably find it difficult to understand how I feel," she continued quietly, "to me we have only buried the husk of the man. I feel him near me, joining with us today and feel comforted by that."

"Er, do you now," O'Mear was thrown off balance by this calm statement. Now what can I say to that? he thought.

Martha saved him the effort. "I may need your advice later. May I come over and see you if I do?"

O'Mear sighed with relief. "To be sure, anytime. Oi'd be delighted to give you any assistance I can."

You silly old devil, don't let her think that you doubt whether they will leave her in this place for long. They'll want the house for the next incumbent. He heard himself offer her shelter in his house at York should it ever chance that she had need, and was surprised once more when she seemed to read his mind and said.

"You never know, we may yet be without a roof over our heads. We could very well take you up on that offer, Father."

Martha turned aside to speak to others now crowding close and O'Mear took the opportunity to return the prayer book to Ted Robinson.

"I hope you don't have trouble for taking a Church of England service here today, Father."

Robinson sounded genuinely concerned, probably worried about his position as a churchwarden here at Bolumbygine.

"Never you worry," said another voice at O'Mear's shoulder. "They won't know, if we don't tell them."

O'Mear turned and saw Fred Sievright, the other warden, standing beside him.

"Thank you Father," he went on. "It was good of you to take the service today, otherwise Ted or I would have had to do so in the absence of any clergy. The rector was a staunch high churchman and would have been very comfortable about the arrangement we came to. Will you come over home now? Mrs Gladwell has not had time to prepare anything, having just got back from York last night. Mrs Robinson and my wife are putting on a light lunch at our house if you would care to join us, please."

The day after the funeral the older children had gone off early to school as usual and Martha, on her hands and knees, was busily engaged in washing the kitchen floor. It was a good job, as she didn't have to think about it, which was just as well when her mind was churning over the problem of what to do next.

Ted Robinson had said that he would write to the bishop on behalf of the Parish Council and ask if she could be allowed to stay on at the rectory for the time being until Robert's affairs were sorted out. Not that that should take long, she thought, as he hadn't very much, just a small sum in credit at the bank in York. His stipend was in arrears as usual. In fact they had never received the full amount in any year since they came. He owned the cow and two of the horses, but the buggy was the property of the church as were the other horses. Robert owned the few old ewes that they had in the paddock to provide them with meat. Her sulky on the other hand was her own property; it had been a gift to her from Robert. The furniture was theirs, and the linen, the piano too, though now she thought about it there was little else.

She stopped scrubbing the last of the floor and sat back on her heels to rest.

There is after all the money in the bank at York that Grandfather Jones left me. She smiled; I still haven't found out how much that amounts to. I suppose I could take the children back to Wiltshire if it would cover the cost of the passage. I must drive into York and find out. You really are scatty, Martha, she told herself and bent down to wipe the suds off the floor.

She had finished the floor and was standing in the doorway, the bucket in her hand surveying her handiwork, when she heard a step on the verandah and, glancing behind her, saw Dora Sievright. Turning, she wiped a lock of hair back from her eyes and smiled at her friend.

"Hello Dora! It's nice to see you and you're just in time for a cup of tea, if you don't mind waiting five minutes while the kitchen floor dries."

"I don't mind waiting at all." Dora sat down on the edge of the verandah and watched as Martha meticulously poured the water remaining in the bucket on the plants against the fence.

"Well, I never got my bathroom or piped water to the house," Martha said, sighing heavily as she returned to the shade of the verandah, "but he was a good husband in spite of that. He just didn't understand what it would have meant to me."

Dora looked at her wonderingly. She had always thought the rector was too selfish by far. He had never given a thought to what Martha needed. When it came to doing the work about the place he had always had his mind on higher things. To be fair though, she admonished herself, he had worked hard enough when he first came to Bolumbygine and no one could gainsay him that he jumped straight in to help Fred and Ted Robinson build the rectory. Once Martha arrived and had taken over the running of the house it was another story and he had sat back whenever he was home and let her wait on him. A wave of irritation flooded over her. It was just like him to die as a result of that silly attempt to stop Charlotte Webb's horses, when everyone knew that Charlotte could handle anything put to a buggy and was probably the best horsewoman in the district. Now Martha was left almost destitute to bring up six children, the youngest not yet a year old.

"Martha," she said sharply. "What are you going to do now?"

Martha didn't immediately answer, but continued drying out the bucket with a cloth and then hung it to dry on the line strung between the verandah posts at the side of the house. Coming back along the verandah she stopped to look down at Dora. "I don't rightly know," she said, breaking into a broad Wiltshire accent for the first time that Dora could remember. She pushed the lock of hair that habitually fell down over her eyes back. "But I tell 'ee, whatever it be, I am not going back to live in t'same house with my Dad and have him preaching at me and my kids."

Dora looked at her friend and thought how pretty she looked, standing there, her chin up, looking her problems in the face.

"Come on, Dora," Martha declared firmly. "What's to be will be and we'll have to make the best of it." Opening the door she beckoned her friend into the kitchen where the kettle was singing merrily on the wood stove.

One evening, two weeks later, Ted Robinson walked over to the Sievright's with a letter from the bishop's secretary.

He stood in their kitchen and, dropping the envelope on the table in front of Fred, invited him to read it.

"Young Mathew was in Beverley this afternoon to see our Sybil down at the school. He picked this up at the post office. It's addressed to us both as churchwardens. I opened it, then thought better of it and brought it over to you so that we could decide how to deal with it." At Dora's invitation he pulled out a chair and sat down.

Fred got to his feet and rummaged for his spectacles on the kitchen dresser. When he had found them he balanced them on his nose and, returning to the table, turned up the wick of the oil lamp and sat down to read.

"Who wrote this letter?" he demanded after a while. "He says that the bishop will decide whether to replace Mr Gladwell but in the meantime we should tell his widow that the church will do whatever it can to help her relocate herself in Perth. Isn't he aware that Martha came out from England? Except for the rector's mother and his brother, who is a partner with Cowan, Dibney and West, she hasn't any family of her own that I know of, in this State or Australia for that matter. What do you think, Dora?"

"I am sure she hasn't any family out here, as she mentioned it today." Dora sat stiffly upright in her chair and looked from one to the other of the two men.

Ted Robinson leaned forward. "If all her people are in England, then I suppose she'll have to go back there. What do you think Fred?"

"Yes, I suppose that would be best," agreed Fred, nodding. Reaching for his tobacco he proceeded to stuff his pipe, then put it in his mouth.

"Where's Martha and the children to live meantime?" asked Dora, standing up and putting a few twigs on the remaining hot coals in the stove. "She'll have to live somewhere and if they aren't going to send another priest for a while it's surely better all round that she continues to stay in the rectory until she knows how much money she has to take passage back to England. If that is what she finally decides to do, " she added.

The twigs broke into flame and Dora took up a poker from the hob at the side and levering out the round hotplate set into the top of the stove, put the kettle over the small fire.

Fred took his pipe out of his mouth and looked at it. "Well, I dunno what she's gunna do," he said, pensively. He peered into the bowl, then pressed the tobacco down with his thumb, before getting up from the table and going over to the stove. He took a small wood spill from a jar on the mantelpiece, lit it, and applied the flame to the pipe. He turned and stood with his back to the fire, puffing.

At last he spoke. "What happens if they don't replace the rector here and decide to put this church into the Beverley parish? They've had a rector at Beverley for several years now. I have never understood why we were part of another group of churches. If they don't replace the rector here then what are they going to do with the rectory? The church owns the few acres surrounding it, but nowhere near enough to support a family if it were farmed. I can't let them have any more land on this side so anyone who wanted it would have to approach Charles Webb. He may be willing to sell the land that adjoins the rectory on the north side. You know the block I am talking about, Ted. It runs back from the river to the top of the ridge. God knows, old Charlie has enough land. Ten and a half thousand acres in all at Broughton, he wouldn't miss a couple of hundred off this end."

"What are you thinking, Fred?" Dora asked quietly. "You surely aren't suggesting that Martha should buy that block from Mr Webb and farm the rectory land."

"No, of course not, no woman could do that, let alone Martha with all those children to bring up. I was just thinking." He paused, then continued deliberately. "If the bishop were to decide not to send us another man, that house would go to rack and ruin if it were left empty for more than a twelve month. I wouldn't like that, Ted. We worked too hard, first to raise the money and then on the building itself, to let it all go for nothing. We would have to find someone to live in it."

He lifted his head and looked at his wife and Ted Robinson in turn. "That's all I have to say," he added shortly.

"I see," she responded briskly. "In the meantime what are you men going to do to help Martha, if she decides not to return to England. Because you can take it from me, she is not very happy at the prospect, even if she did have the money for the passage, which I am sure she hasn't."

Dora stood up with her hands on her hips and regarded them sternly, looking at her husband first and then, when she couldn't catch his eye, at their neighbour.

Ted stole a glance at her, then, quickly lowering his eyes before her gaze, he mumbled. "I dunno. What do you suggest we do, have a round robin amongst the congregations that he used to go to? I suppose we could do that; might raise some money for her passage that way."

"Yes, I think that is the least the people of this parish can do."

Dora stood her ground, daring either of them to disagree with her.

****

Chapter 10
Dora's solution

The boards of the back verandah of the Sievright home creaked, and a knock and a cheerful coo-ee were followed by footsteps in the passage.

"Come in Martha," Dora called. "How did it go?" she enquired as her friend appeared at the kitchen door.

"Much better than ever I had expected, Dora," Martha said excitedly. "When I arrived in York and found that the bank manager was out again I was quite depressed, but after waiting outside his office for half an hour he came in and saw me immediately. Dora, my grandfather left me enough money to take us all back to England, if we have to go."

"I am so glad for you, that must be a big worry off your mind. But what will you do when you get there?" Dora looked at her steadily.

"That is the question. I don't know. My father and I don't get on and in any case it wouldn't be fair to land on my mother with six small children. I would have to find some way of making a living." Martha sat down at the table. "What do you suggest, Dora?"

"Don't do anything just for the moment. You have enough to live on for several months, so stay here and see what develops. I have an idea that I want to sound out with someone else before I tell you about it, as I don't want to raise false hopes. I need time to work it out," Dora said thoughtfully, "and then I promise you that I will explain what is in my mind. There is no harm done if you go slowly. The children will get over the shock of their father's death easier if they are in familiar surroundings and in any case the bishop appears to be in no hurry to send a man up here."

She turned to the stove and, picking up the kettle, poured hot water into the tea pot to warm it.

Martha lay in the centre of the big brass bed listening to the quiet breathing of Timothy in his cot by the wall. It was a still night and all was quiet, apart from the dull clang of a Condamine bell on one of the horses in the paddock and the sound of a cricket somewhere in the house. Perspiring in her light cotton night gown she wondered whether she should put a stretcher bed on the verandah and sleep out there with the older children. Robert had always been insistent that they should sleep in the privacy of their bedroom. Now it was entirely up to her what she did she mused, and resolved to move to the side verandah the next day and gain the benefit of any breeze.

The baby moved restlessly then turned over with a sigh. Martha spread her arms and legs starfish fashion and lay on the bottom sheet with her bed clothes thrown aside, thinking of the options open to her. There were not many she concluded. She had no desire to go home to Wiltshire where she would be subject to the pressure of her father's rigid ideas. She loved her mother dearly and had no wish to hurt her but had little in common with her brother Tom who was still living at home, or Ailine for that matter. She smiled. Her sister had gone to work for her grandfather in his office and, to her father's disgust, on his death she had inherited his substantial house in the town.

If only George was older, we could use grandfather's legacy to buy a small farm, but you cannot expect a boy of nine to work a farm, she told herself. He had to go to school. If they moved into Beverley perhaps they could find a house to rent. There were several houses unoccupied since the Government of West Australia had purchased the Great Southern Railway from its shareholders and there had been less need for so many railway men in the town. The trains from Albany ran through to Perth nowadays, instead of the passengers being forced to change at Beverley.

Her brother-in-law, William Gladwell, had written to say that there could be a small pension payable by the church to her as the widow of a clergyman. He had also suggested that if her legacy was invested in Government Stock she would be able to manage in a country town where many of the costs were less than in Perth. Perhaps, she mused, she should go and see the bishop and ask him what was planned and how long she could remain at the rectory. After all, she had had no official word from his office except a brief acknowledgement to her letter advising the bishop of Robert's death.

Martha thought she would discuss this plan with Dora and if she was willing to look after the children for two or three days a letter could be sent to the bishop requesting an appointment. He would hardly be likely to refuse her and perhaps would offer to pay her train fare.

Martha smiled sleepily; necessity was making her take a business like approach to managing her affairs. Whatever would Robert be thinking of her, she wondered. Feeling the first touch of a breeze she turned over and went to sleep.

A week later Martha was in her front garden putting some of her precious laundry water on the flowering bushes. Hearing the sound of a horse trotting down the hill she looked up and recognised Charlotte Webb in the distance, riding a fine chestnut down the track past the church. She emptied the last of the water out of the bucket, turned and went inside the kitchen to finish her chores.

She was sweeping the side verandah, perhaps a half an hour later, when she saw Charlotte leading her horse, walking with Dora through the trees towards the rectory.

Martha laid her straw broom against the wall and went into the house to tidy her hair and put the kettle on. By the time the two women reached the rectory, Martha was waiting for them out at the gate.

Dora spoke first: "I've brought Charlotte to see you, Martha. She has a proposal to make that you may find interesting."

Martha looked enquiringly at Dora and then at Charlotte, beautifully turned out as always, not a hair out of place.

Charlotte regarded her kindly with those odd green eyes of hers from under her wide hat. She spoke diffidently. " It is only that we are having a lot of bother with the sheep at this end of the run, Martha. When I mentioned this to Dora today, she said that perhaps you might have some interest in acquiring some additional land. I thought my father-in-law would perhaps be happy to be rid of the problem and he could let you have the four hundred-acres that adjoins this property. It is good land and some of it is partly cleared, but it is detached from the rest of Broughton by that strip of Crown Land that takes in the top of the ridge. This creates a problem for us in handling our sheep. This is especially so since the wool market declined and Mr Webb plans to reduce the number of shepherds on the place and will rely on wire fences in the future."

Martha's mind raced. Does that mean that he would be willing to let me buy it, she wondered. Perhaps if that block were joined to the thirty acres around the Rectory I would then have enough to make a living from the land here. The problem is that the church owns the rectory, I don't.

Dora watching her closely saw the look of hope on her friend's face and said practically, "May we come in and have a cup of tea, Martha. I'm sure you have one ready and then if we sit around the table together, we can talk over Charlotte's suggestion and see if we can't work something out."

Martha felt slightly flustered at having to consider this proposal without prior warning, but was quickly put at ease by Charlotte who showed an immediate interest in the baby Tim, who was lying in his cot in the nursery laughing and crowing.

Once they were sitting at the kitchen table she was able to give her undivided attention to Charlotte as she explained her plan.

If Martha was interested in the land, Charlotte said, she would approach her father-in-law and ask him if he would be willing to sell it to Martha with payment deferred over a number of years. Laughing charmingly, Charlotte said that having raised the subject she would wait and let the idea sink in as he would probably protest that women couldn't run a farm, even though he was the first to acknowledge that his wife had more or less run Broughton at one stage. Once he had absorbed the basic idea, she would suggest that he should first approach the bishop in Perth and see if the church would be willing to sell Martha the rectory and its surrounding land on similar terms.

Martha explained that she had written to the bishop and had asked for an appointment, but hadn't had a reply from his secretary as yet.

Charlotte smiled and said she would tell her father-in-law that Martha was going to see the bishop and that she would perhaps be happy if he accompanied her.

The three women talked this over at length and eventually it was decided that Charlotte would discuss the matter with Mr Webb and if she obtained a favourable response then she would arrange for Martha to meet him to discuss it further.

It being agreed, Charlotte stood up saying it was time for her to be off back to Broughton. She thanked Martha for the tea, said goodbye and rode off after promising to let her know within a day or so how Charles Webb received the idea.

Charlotte did write Martha a note within a few days, but it was her father-in-law, Charles Webb himself who brought it over to Bolumbygine, riding his elderly grey thoroughbred.

Martha was on the wood heap cutting firewood and didn't see him approach until he had dismounted and tied his horse up in the shade of the gum tree at the back of the house.

He saw a neat little woman, wearing a clean apron over her

blouse and skirt, picking up firewood. He couldn't at first see her face as it was in the shade of her poke bonnet, but when she did look up at him full faced he was surprised how young she was.

Never readily at ease when alone with a young woman, he cleared his throat and barked. "Ahem! Mrs Gladwell, I am sorry that I have never met you before, but I am Charles Webb. I did meet your husband some time ago, but these days I am more or less retired from the active management of Broughton which I nowadays leave to my son Harry, while my wife Clara and I live in Guildford for the greater part of the year."

Martha was surprised at his manner of speech, which was gruff and almost abrupt. Realising he was shy, she smiled over the armful of firewood that she clasped to her chest and with difficulty held out her hand.

"Good morning Mr Webb," she said. "I have met your daughter-in-law you know."

"Yes, I do know and that is why I am here today. I have a letter to you from her. She wants you to bring your children and to come over for lunch on Sunday, but you had better read it yourself."

He scrabbled in his pockets, turning them out into his hand like a small boy, before he found what he wanted and handed her a small violet coloured envelope. She couldn't hold it properly because of the wood, and dropped it.

When he had recovered the note, she said. "I am sorry, my hands are full. Would you come into the house please and I will drop this wood into the wood box. Perhaps you will allow me to give you a cup of tea. Could you bring one or two extra pieces with you please," she added, not wishing to waste his potential.

Charles Webb picked up another armful of wood and wonderingly followed the small figure on to the verandah and into the house where, having dropped the load she carried into the wood box, she took off her bonnet, shook out her hair and moved across to the stove.

"Please make yourself at home, Mr Webb," she said brightly. "Please sit down at the table, at the head there, and I'll make us some tea."

He sat and, looking around him, noted that the floor was scrubbed and everything in the small room was neat and clean as a new pin, as he related to his wife later.

Martha quickly laid the table and put out freshly made bread rolls and some butter from Robert's cool cupboard on the verandah.

"Who do you have to help you, Mrs Gladwell?" he asked, as he leaned forward to take a roll from the full plate she offered him.

"Only the children. George, who is nine and Elizabeth, two years younger, are both a wonderful help, especially Elizabeth who looks after the younger children when she is at home."

"Where are they now?" he enquired, spreading the bread with jam.

"The older children are at school, in Beverley. The baby, Timothy, and our younger daughter Rebecca are still at home. They are very good."

"But Beverley is seven or eight miles from here, that's a long way. How do they go, or does someone pick them up?" he asked, as he bit into the crisp bread roll, and tried to work out how one person could manage this number of children.

"Not quite as far as that across country. The children walk. Their father was always insistent that they should attend school regularly and while he was rarely here, because his parish covered a large area, the children are very proud of the fact that they have never missed a single day at school, winter or summer, which proves it's healthy, walking to and fro, night and morning."

"Fourteen miles a day," he said wonderingly, his mouth full of roll and jam, which in part he had transferred to his white moustache. A thought seemed to strike him. "That is a very long way in this day and age."

"Yes, I agree, but we have no choice, as their father was often away for three weeks at a time around the parish with his buggy and pair. They have all come to accept that they have chores to do, including the little ones. Robert said it was character building."

She smiled and offered him another cup of tea and another bread roll, which he accepted readily.

Gladwell seems to have been free with his wisdom, he thought. I hope he was as ready to help this remarkable young lady when he was at home. Most of the clergy I have met have little enough to do except visit their parishioners and to take a couple of services on a Sunday. He looked up into a pair of eyes dancing with fun.

"Well," he said. "I am certainly glad that I have met you at last, in spite of the delay. I do hope that you will all come over to lunch on Sunday and meet Clara. She'll like you." He finished his tea and, taking out a large white handkerchief, wiped his moustache. He looked around him, found his hat on the floor beside his chair and standing, pulled out a gold pocket watch.

He peered at it, then put it away again. "Must be going. Thank you for the tea and for the bread rolls, Mrs Gladwell. They were very good."

Martha saw him to the gate and shook hands with him. He was surprised to find that she had a firm grip, like a man.

He stalked to where his horse was tethered under the pepper tree and mounted stiffly. Then, as though a thought struck him, he turned the horse and rode back to where she was still standing at the gate.

"Mrs Gladwell, it was very pleasant to talk to you. Charlotte had told me that I would enjoy meeting you. I think you and I will be able to work something out regarding the land that will be satisfactory to you and the children. If you don't mind I would like to have a private word with the bishop before we see him together. You had better let me know when that's to be when you come over to Broughton. Goodbye, Mrs Gladwell, I look forward to seeing you on Sunday."

With old fashioned courtesy he took off his hat and bowed his head slightly to her, before neck reining the horse away. He rode off, sitting very straight in his saddle.

On Sunday Martha enjoyed the luxury of having a meal she hadn't cooked placed before her. She also enjoyed meeting the rest of the Webbs, especially Mrs Clara Webb whom she had heard was a strong willed woman, but with whom she quickly found common ground.

She was less impressed with Charlotte's husband Harry, who seemed to spend all his time ogling the young maid who waited at the luncheon table. Charlotte's boys Thomas, Desmond and Charles, a little older than her own, she liked. If the girls Victoria (Vicky) and Sarah (Sally) appeared pampered and a little precious, well, that wasn't her business.

She had a short conversation with Mr Webb before lunch at which it was tacitly agreed that they would meet the bishop the following week. Apart from that, nothing more was said about her buying the land adjoining the rectory, except that as they were all saying goodbye and the children were climbing into the sulky, Charlotte said. "I am glad we have that fixed up. I'll be over to see you during the week, Martha."

Then they were driving away down the road through the old white gums and past the shearing shed and other buildings.

The meeting with the bishop went off very well. Martha was initially surprised to find this large and slightly fierce looking man could be so gentle. She was delighted to learn that he was resolved that in future Bolumbygine would become part of the Beverley parish. He told her too that as she was already living in the Rectory she would be given first opportunity to buy it at cost or valuation, whichever the Diocesan Council agreed.

At this point Charles Webb had looked very hard at the bishop. He told him that he would be extremely fortunate to find a buyer for the Rectory, situated as it was miles from the nearest township and with insufficient land to make it a viable proposition as a farm. The bishop had come up short at that but finally agreed to put before the Diocesan Council a proposal to sell the property to Martha at a valuation to be provided by a sworn valuator recommended by Mr Webb.

As they left the bishop's house Charles Webb rubbed his hands in satisfaction. "A very good day's business, Mrs Gladwell," he said. "You may be sure that we will secure the house for you at the value of the building for removal to another site. As for the land, well there is no water on that block so it won't be worth very much. Which reminds me, whatever got into Robinson and Sievright? Any new chum would know that it was quite impractical to site a house on the top of a hill like that, rather than down by the river where there was a chance of finding water. Very important to have a good supply of water, Mrs Gladwell."

He continued to talk in this fashion as the horse cab took them along St Georges Terrace from the bishop's house to the Palace Hotel for lunch.

****

CHAPTER 11
Crisis, April 1906

"It's got to stop Martha. You can't expect us to go on providing for you and your tribe as we have these last four years." Edith Robinson's voice rose as she spat out the words.

"But I've paid whatever was asked, for the work your sons have done. I paid Mathew for shearing the sheep." Martha was horrified at this outburst from her neighbour.

Edith looked at her venomously. "You've never paid more than a pittance for all the work they've done." She took a step forward across the rectory kitchen floor. "Fluttered your eyelashes at them more like. They're all besotted with you. Even Ted, poor fool that he is. Poor little woman, brave little woman," she sneered. "I am sick of it. Who built this house for the church, I ask you? We did, but it was you and Charles Webb who persuaded the bishop to let you have it for next to nothing. The people of this parish raised the money for you to send your boy to school in Perth. Nobody ever offered to send our sons to private schools. Knowing you, it is just as well that the bishop holds that money in trust or you would have spent it on this place. You were left all that money by your grandfather and you persuaded Charles Webb, silly old fool that he is, to sell you that block cheap. Now you are friendlier with the Webbs and dear Dora of course, than you are with us, who have done all your work for you. Not good enough for the likes of you, I suppose, even though you told me a long time ago that your own father was chapel. Trying to rise above your station, that's what you're doing."

Martha had turned white during this outpouring of vitriol, her knuckles gleaming as she held on to the chair, her back to the stove.

"You are twisting everything, you must be sick, Edith," she said in a low voice.

Edith's face contorted and her voice rose to a screech. "Don't tell me I'm sick. You scarlet woman. You were carousing in that hospital with those railway workers the night your poor husband died. There was plenty of talk about that at the time, I can tell you." Narrowing her eyes she came a step closer. "Look at the friends you have now. Charlotte Webb is nothing but a high-class tart with her weekend visitors and the gentlemen from Perth and Northam who stay overnight, whenever the old people are away at Guildford. They certainly don't go there to see Harry Webb, not that he is ever there. He's off at the races or chasing that barmaid at the Settlers' Arms in Beverley. Who could blame him, when his wife behaves the way she does."

Martha's shoulders shook. "Don't go on, please don't go on. You know its untrue and you must not say such things."

Edith mimicked her. "Don't say such things Edith, you mustn't. Why shouldn't I? Dear Dora comes up here and tells you all the gossip and she's a liar if ever there was one. She was always my friend until you came here; you turned her against me. I wish you had never come here, you and Robert, that lovely, lovely man you drove away from me. We were all so happy when he first came here and he used to come down every night for his dinner and tell me all his problems. But it was all spoilt when you arrived."

She stopped, realising that she had finally gone too far, her hand to her mouth, her face appalled at what she had said. Then tossing her head she tried to brazen it out. "Well, it had to be said. I could have taken Robert away from you had I wished, but I couldn't be bothered." She shrugged her shoulders. "So don't try to take Ted away from me now, because it won't do you any good."

Martha stood there, her eyes wide, looking at the woman before her, unable to believe what she was hearing.

Edith lifted her hand menacingly, her face livid with rage. "There, that'll give you something to talk about with dear Dora won't it. That other bitch, too. The three bitches will have plenty to get their heads together about now, won't they? If you dare!" Edith shouted, and she spat at Martha. "That is what I think of you. Scum, all of you."

She turned and marched out of the house. Martha, tears streaming down her face, remained standing in front of the stove, her hands still gripping the back of the chair. Taking the handkerchief from her sleeve she dried her eyes and seeing the spittle on her apron, she shuddered and wiped it away.

She opened the doors of the firebox at the top of the stove and pushed the coals together. With a sob, she lifted the round plate out and placed the kettle over the flames where it commenced to sing. Remaining leaning over the stove, her hand holding onto the mantelshelf, she felt more alone than she had ever been in her life.

As he drove through the trees Father O'Mear could see that the land had been cleared from the edge of the ridge up to the hill above the Bolumbygine church. A large part was divided into two paddocks by Harper fences, the rest cropped or grazed by shepherded sheep. Hearing the plunk of an axe close by, he looked to his right and saw a young boy cutting a fallen sapling into lengths of about six feet. He pulled up his horse and sat there watching the lad at his work.

A voice spoke from the other side of the road. "Hello, Father. We haven't seen you for a while. Will you have some lunch with us?"

The priest turned his head and did not at first see the woman kneeling on an old sack by a hole in the ground, a jam tin in her hand that she had been using to dig.

"How are you Mrs Gladwell? What are you doing there?"

"Putting up a few more panels of fencing to keep our sheep in."

She picked up the short steel bar that she had been using to loosen the ground in the bottom of the hole and ramming it into the earth, hung the tin on it. Standing up she pushed a lock of hair back over her head with a grubby hand, and walked to the buggy, picking her way carefully over ground littered with the sticks and leaves of past seasons.

Standing beside him, she looked up. "Could you spare me some time, Father? I have a problem and would be glad of your advice."

"Why to be sure," he said kindly. " I have been to visit some of my parishioners who work for Mr Webb and thought I would come around this way to Beverley to see the new man there. I was hoping I would catch sight of you as I had heard that you were having a hard time out here, what with the poor season and the low prices for wheat and wool."

"We manage." Martha rejoined. "If you will stop and have a bite with us, I'll come to the house now." She raised her voice and called to the boy, who was dragging the lengths of timber he had cut, across to the fence line.

"George, Father O'Mear is going to have lunch with us. I'll go up to the house with him and put the kettle on. Will you come up in about half an hour?"

"I'll be there. Good to see you Father." The boy called, and returned to his work.

Martha scrambled nimbly up to join O'Mear on the seat of the buggy and they set off down the road towards the low ridge where the rectory stood.

Neither spoke until they had crested the rise above the church. Then Martha turned to the priest and in an urgent voice said. "Father, it is so difficult to know what to do for the best."

He turned and smiled encouragingly. "My dear," he said, "you are raising a good Christian family, there is no better thing in the eyes of God. Look at that lad we have just left, George. He's a good boy."

"Yes, he is a good boy, that's true, but I don't know what I'll do when he goes to Mr Harper's school at Guildford in May. We still have to put the crop in and I can't go on accepting the charity of my neighbours to do the cropping year after year."

The priest reined the horse around into the track that ran up to the Rectory. "I thought your neighbour's boys were helping you with the heavy work?"

"So they were," she said bitterly, "but Mrs Robinson has been up to see me and has told me that she believes I'm contaminating her sons and trying to make off with her husband. I can't rely for help from that quarter. Mr and Mrs Sievright and their family have been wonderful, but I can't go on accepting their help."

"That's too bad, Mrs Gladwell, though I can understand how such a problem can come about in a small community like this." He was silent a minute, shaking his head as he pondered the problem.

Martha said nothing, contenting herself with looking ahead of the horse as it plodded its way toward the rear of the house.

O'Mear sighed, then said, "Let me see if I can come up with something." He looked at her and smiled sympathetically. "It is never so bad as it seems, you know, even when you feel the tongues are clacking away. If you ignore them, after a while they'll stop out of boredom and turn their attention to somebody else."

They pulled up by the gate and Martha climbed down. Looking up to him, tears coursing down her cheeks, she said: "I do hope that you are right, Father, because I can't go and hide anywhere. This is my home and all I possess in the world." She continued to look unhappily into his kind face, then gave a small smile. "I'll run in and wash my face, and send the boys out to help you feed and water your horse."

O'Mear jumped to the ground and, grasping the horse's bit, backed the buggy around to park it in the shade of the tree by the back gate. Two small boys suddenly materialised beside him and helped him take the horse out of the shafts.

"And what are your names?" he asked.

"He's Douglas and I am Anthony," answered the shorter of the pair, a curly haired urchin of about nine.

"How are you Anthony, and you too Douglas?" asked the priest politely. "You know something, I've seen you before. Certainly I have seen you, Douglas."

They both looked at him warily.

"I'm Father O'Mear. I live in York."

Curiosity overcame Anthony's politeness. "Are you a real father?" He asked, squinting as he looked at the priest.

"Yes, a shepherd of my flock." O'Mear answered.

Anthony scuffed his bare foot in the dirt, then looked up at the big man.

"But you haven't a wife have you?"

O'Mear laughed delightedly, "No, that is true, but you can still be a father to your flock you know."

****

CHAPTER 12
Father O'Mear provides help

The rains that year were early and a few days after the first heavy showers Elizabeth was up at the stable sitting on the top rail of the horse yard swinging her legs, the other children playing around the building.

A flurry amongst the galahs that inhabited the trees down by the road attracted her attention. Under the circling cloud of pink and grey parrots she caught sight of two men swinging up the track towards her with their swags on their backs. She called out to them and waved. One of the men stopped and pointed her out to his companion.

"Your mother anywhere around?" he asked as they came up to her.

"Yes, she's over there with my brother George; they're putting up a new fence for the sheep." Elizabeth slid down from the rail and taking a few steps to the side of the building pointed along the river.

"Mind if we leave our swags here while we go down and see her?" asked the other man, who had fair hair and a sandy coloured beard.

"That's all right. You can put them in here," she said, pointing into the feed room. "I'll tell the others not to touch them. Shall I send Douglas with you, to show you where mother and George are?"

"It might be an idea if you did," said the first man, who had a thick brown beard, and kind eyes. A white line of scar tissue pulled his right eyebrow upward to give him a permanent air of interrogation.

The men placed their swags against the wall in the feed room and set off down the paddock with Douglas skipping along ahead of them. Reaching the division fence made of horizontal rails laid between two posts set firmly in the ground, the man with the dark beard lifted Douglas over then, putting one hand on a post vaulted it. The blonde man backed up the hill and with a shout ran towards the fence and leaped over it.

The older man laughed, "You're full of the joys of spring today, Billy boy."

"And why not Arthur? It has been a hard year and now that we've sold the mine, we deserve a break before we get down to serious business again." He grinned and suddenly looked much younger.

They walked to where Martha and George were building the boundary fence, with rails laid between pairs of posts, Harper fashion, along the side of the road.

Martha had seen the men coming down the hill from the sheds and had finished arranging the last of the rails between the uprights as they came up to her.

"Mummy, these men wanted to see you. Elizabeth sent me down with them." Douglas called as he danced along, jumping onto a fallen log that lay across the fence line, then off again. "George, what have you got there?" he demanded, seeing something hanging from a tree."

"A rabbit, silly. I snared it last night," his elder brother answered in quelling tones.

Martha turned to the men, both dressed in working clothes, dark tweed trousers and grey flannel shirts, but not otherwise alike. The younger man fair-haired with blue eyes and a happy mobile face was vaguely familiar. The other, more her own age, with a long intelligent face and kind brown eyes, removed his hat, revealing dark hair streaked with grey receding from a high forehead.

"Mrs Gladwell?" he enquired in a soft voice with a distinct burr in it. "I'm Arthur Trevylian and this is my mate, Bill Pederick. Father O'Mear told us to tell you that he sent us out. We're looking for a place to camp for a few days and he thought you may be willing for us to doss down in your stable now it's coming on a bit colder. We would be happy to do some work for your kindness. We're both handy and strong. I'm not so bad with horses and Billy is a rare shearer with the blades."

Martha looked from one to the other. "Well, George has to go off to school next week, so I certainly need a hand to put in the crop, and for shearing too, but I have no money to pay you."

Bill smiled his face lighting up. "We don't need no money, Ma'am. We've been working in the mines at Coolgardie and at Hannan's these last few years and what we need is a break. They say a change is as good as a holiday and your place is far enough from any pub for the drink not to be tempting us."

"Yes," added Arthur seeing the frown on Martha's face. "We don't want to throw away money it has taken us so long to earn. We've made that mistake before and by the time we changed our cheques at the pub and the publican gave us his shin plasters for them, made of blotting paper they were and what with the sweat of your hands, it were no time before they fell apart. Then we had no choice but to go back to the mine. This time we decided not to accept PN's, promissory notes that is, and we had our money sent down to the West Australian Bank at York while we came down quiet and sober to see Father O'Mear and get his advice what to do. An' that's how we come to be here now."

"Father O'Mear said we had to get used to the idea that we had some capital and work out what we were going to do with it, while we are here." Bill added. "And he said you would maybe give us some work and perhaps some bread and mutton, which would be a rare change from the salt beef and damper we've been eating up on the Goldfields."

Martha made up her mind. She liked the openness of these men, and she smiled. "Well, if Father O'Mear recommends you, you can sleep in the shed; it is at least dry and the horses keep it warm in winter. But you mustn't light a fire or smoke tobacco in there. That must be clearly understood from the start as I couldn't afford to have it burned down. No drinking alcohol either, please. If you will help me around the farm I'll feed you. It'll be plain cooking mind but probably no worse than you're used to. Now, let's make that a bargain."

She offered her hand and shook theirs solemnly as she had seen farmers do in the market place at Warminster when she was a young girl.

The two men moved into the shed and made the hay loft their home. Martha told the children that they were to respect their privacy and stay close to the house. She gave them a hurricane lantern for use in the evening and fed them three meals a day. For their part they quickly took charge of the work on the farm and Arthur Trevylian was true to his word that he was good with horses and shortly after they had arrived he went off to Beverley one day and returned with four heavy shire horses.

"Where did you get those horses, Mr Trevylian?" Martha asked when he came up to get their evening meal.

He took off his hat and looked at her. "I am sorry that I didn't ask your permission, Mrs Gladwell, but I've been thinking that Billy and me will need good horses for our new business. Ted Robinson told me that you usually borrow his, but due to him having a spot of bother with some of them being footsore he can't help you this year. So having the opportunity to buy some real nice young stock, I snapped them up. They're good animals and I couldn't afford to miss them. They'll suit Billy and me right well. If you don't mind I could put them to the plough here and break them in like; they need the work. You would be doing us a favour." He raised his eyes and looked at her trustingly.

Martha was unsure what she should do but she certainly needed heavy horses to put in the crop if Edith was forcing Ted not to lend her a team. She had a vague feeling that it was all being sorted out too easily, but put that behind her.

"Thank you Mr Trevylian, that'll be a big help. I'll have plenty of feed for them, that's one good thing, as I always feed Mr Robinson's horses through the winter in exchange for having the use of them."

Arthur went off with the food on a tray to the feed room where he and Billy had rigged up a few planks as a table.

Bill looked up as he pushed the door open. "Was she happy about the horses?"

"I think so. But she hasn't much alternative has she," he straightened and looked across at his friend. "She's a game little body, Billy. Them kids are nicely brought up, real well behaved they are. Can't have been easy with the reverend dead, but we'll be able to give her a good start this year."

He pulled a rough bench made from a Jarrah plank nailed to two kerosene boxes from under the trestle table and started to pour the tea.

Martha had enough to worry about that autumn and winter. George went off to Mr Harper's school at Guildford from where he wrote imploring letters asking to be allowed to come home. He wasn't a big boy or a good scholar and suffered miserably from the bullying of the other boys at the school. When he came home for the August holidays he was desperate and pleaded with her not to send him back.

Taking advantage of the early season Arthur Trevylian had ploughed all the ground to be cropped using one of a Beverley farmer's newly invented stump jump ploughs that he had purchased as an investment, or so he informed Martha. She was so worried about George at the time that she never thought to question the use that Arthur and Billy would have for a four-furrow plough in their proposed transport business.

The two men kept to themselves and though Martha worried about them living in the shed she realised that it was wiser to keep them at arms length. She meanwhile busied herself with looking after the smaller children and with cutting down some of Robert's old clerical suits to make shorts for the boys. In all of this she enjoyed the support of Dora and Fred Sievright, who continued to encourage her with the farm in every way they could.

The breach with Edith however, was now an acknowledged fact. When she met Ted Robinson on the track down to Sievrights he was always polite and friendly, but he appeared ill at ease at church for the monthly service when other people were present.

Dora told her to take no notice. Edith had always been jealous of other people. It wasn't, she said, that Ted didn't provide for her, for they were well off financially, but Edith had never been any different and always envied other's possessions.

"It's plain, she was born envious; it's a disease that eats her soul away," said Dora philosophically. "There is nothing you can do to help her, except to go on treating her as though nothing has changed. The Lord knows I have put up with her ways for more than twenty-five years. Edith will always be a troublemaker, even though, in fairness to her, when there is a real disaster she's the first to man the pump."

Arthur and Billy set up a rough lean-to against the side of the stable to serve as a shearing board and thatched it with ti-tree brought up from the river. They built a small pen for the sheep and laid a floor of rough sawn Wandoo face cuts that they obtained from the sawmill at Dale River.

Using old discarded hand shears, over which they lavished great care to reset and to sharpen to a keen edge, they shore the sheep. Martha and Elizabeth helped them, picking up the fleeces as they were shorn and skirting them of sweat stained pieces. Having sorted the wool by length and fineness of staple, Martha packed it into big chaff bags. Elizabeth swept the floor between sheep to keep it clear of second cuts and stained pieces that fell out of the shorn fleece, dashing to one or other with a rag swab dipped in Stockholm Tar to dress the occasional cut when they called 'Tar-boy'.

Shearing over, Arthur came down to the house one afternoon when the children were at school, knocked at the door, and entered the kitchen at Martha's call.

"Hello, Mr Trevylian, is everything all right?" she asked, looking up from the table where she was writing.

Arthur stood just inside the door and looked down at her. "It's time that we went about our business, Mrs Gladwell. Billy is going to walk into Beverley in the morning and will catch the train to York. He's going to arrange with the bank manager there to give him a letter to his Head Office in Perth and will then go down and find someone who can build us two or three good sized wagons."

Martha propped her head on her hands and looked up at him, her head on one side, quite unconscious of the appealing picture she presented to the lonely man.

"What are you planning to do after that?" she asked.

"There is a lot going on up at the Goldfields but there is still a tremendous problem with transport, not only to carry stores out to the mines, but also to take the ore that is dug out of the smaller workings to the state batteries to be crushed. Billy and I have some ideas about the type of wagon required. We have talked it over often enough since we've been here and I think we've got it right now. Billy is going to arrange for one wagon to be built as a start and then if that turns out well we will have the others built. I'll stay up here and if it is all right with you, I'll go around the farms and buy some good horses. There appears to be plenty around Beverley and York, which is just as well as we are going to need half a dozen teams."

"What about the team you have here now?"

"That is what I wanted to discuss with you. May we keep our horses here? We need a depot somewhere to rest them from time to time. Of course we would pay you for their feed and grazing. My idea is that we will keep changing the teams regularly as they get leg weary on the hard ground and need a good spell from time to time. If you would be agreeable that is. We'd be willing to pay well."

"Of course I'm agreeable if we can work out a fair thing to cover the cost of feed and pasture. It would be an enormous help to have a regular income, but couldn't you find another more suitable place for your depot, perhaps closer to the railway at Northam or somewhere?"

"No," he said firmly. "That wouldn't suit me at all. I would like to be able to come back to see how the children are getting on and keep an eye on you all."

"But why would you want to do that, Mr Trevylian?" Martha asked quietly, looking at his kind face as he shifted his feet in his embarrassment.

"Oh, nothing. I just want that you and the children will be comfortable. I'll be off now and tell Billy that you're agreeable to our plan."

He turned around and bolted out of the house and across the verandah, leaving her staring after him, a surprised look on her face that slowly softened.

After Bill Pederick departed for Perth, Arthur continued to extend the Harper rail fences until three paddocks had been enclosed for the sheep. Martha worked with him when she could and there grew a close companionship between them which both found more precious than they would admit.

Arthur grumbled. "You shouldn't be down here working with me, Mrs Gladwell. That Edith Robinson is always coming up the road to the top of the hill to spy on you. I don't want her to be giving you a bad name to the neighbours."

Martha didn't pause from her task of fitting the rails he had cut between the upright posts. "Bunnies to Mrs Robinson," she said gaily. "It's my property and I have every right to work on it and with whom so ever I wish. I enjoy working with you."

He stopped and looked at her, then said slowly. "I can't bear to think of you alone with the children, battling on with this place. Why don't you lease it to Fred Sievright, he'd be glad to have it, now his boys are growing up? You could bring the children and come with me up to Kalgoorlie."

Martha stopped short and looked at him. "What are you suggesting, Mr Trevylian? That I come as housekeeper. With six children. Are you mad?"

"No, I'm not," he said quietly. "I don't think you should be on your own out here in the bush. It is too hard a life for someone gently brought up. I want to take care of you Mrs Gladwell and the children. I want you to marry me."

"You don't know what you are saying," she said shortly. "It's a big responsibility taking on a woman with six children. I wouldn't want to land that sort of millstone around any man's neck, least of all someone as decent as you."

He took a few steps towards her, his voice rough with emotion. "Why not? I'd be a good father to them, they need a father too, you shouldn't deny them that."

"I have no intention of getting married again. We've managed very well so far. It's not been easy, I'd be the first to admit that, but we haven't starved yet."

"But what about yourself," he persisted, coming closer. "Don't you wish you had a shoulder to lean on and a hand around your waist sometimes?" He slipped his arm around her as he said this.

For a moment she leaned against him, then jumped as though burned and ran away from him before turning.

"Mr Trevylian, how dare you. No, I don't need a man in the way you put it. I made a resolve when Robert, Mr Gladwell that is, died, not to take another man, but to bring the children up in his memory. In any case," she added, intent on being honest with him. "I had had enough of being left responsible for looking after the children for weeks on end while Robert was away around his parish. I was always expected to be loving whenever my husband chose to return, regardless of any difficulty that I may have encountered in his absence, none of which appeared to be of importance compared with his work."

"But Mrs Gladwell, that is not what it would be like with me."

"The answer is no, Mr Trevylian. I know little about you and I am not going to risk it for my own sake this time, let alone for the children. I value my freedom and I intend to keep it."

She turned and walked off up the hill, slowly at first, as she half expected him to run after her and talk her out of her decision. But he didn't do that and as she climbed towards the house she became conscious of the hurt she had done him. He was clearly not a man who made such an offer without thinking about it carefully and having been rejected was not likely to repeat it.

Martha stayed in the house for the rest of the afternoon and it wasn't until Douglas came in with a brief note that she realised that Arthur had packed his swag and had gone. She ran to the shed, and climbed up to the hayloft where they had lived, but it was empty. It was spotlessly clean, the plates and other utensils washed up and lying on the table.

"Oh, Arthur," she breathed and, going to the shuttered window, looked out down the river and towards York, but couldn't see him.

There was a flurry of movement below. "Mother, Rebecca's been bitten by a snake." Elizabeth's panic stricken voice called out. "Please come quickly!"

Martha ran to the loft ladder and hurried down.

****

CHAPTER 13
The low point

When Martha reached the house she found Rebecca lying on the ground near the wood heap, George sitting beside her, his hands around the top of her leg as he tried to keep his thumbs pressed on the pressure point in her thigh.

Martha took in the scene at a glance and sent Elizabeth to get the medicine case.

"Where did the snake bite her, George?" she asked quietly.

"Down there by the foot, Mum," he said, indicating the direction with his chin.

The two puncture wounds caused by the snake's fangs were clearly discernible below the child's ankle. Martha nodded. "I can see them now. I'll go and get something to deal with it," and she ran into the house.

Taking up the sharp knife they used for killing sheep, a length of twine and a stick from the firewood box by the stove, she was back beside George in less than a minute. She rapidly wound the twine around the upper part of Rebecca's leg as a tourniquet then inserted the piece of firewood and twisted it in the now thick rope of twine to apply pressure, securing it so that it couldn't unravel. Telling Elizabeth to place the medical case beside her and George to hold Rebecca., Martha made an incision between the two puncture wounds and, bending forward, sucked it with her mouth before spitting the blood and venom onto the ground. She repeated this several times, released the tourniquet for a while, then tightened it again. She shook Condy's Crystals into the wound and covered it with a clean handkerchief that the ever-resourceful Elizabeth had produced from her sleeve. Rebecca was almost comatose by this time and clearly very ill.

Martha carried her into the house, calling to George to catch the horse and to put it to the sulky.

Knowing that Dora had planned to go to York that day she told Elizabeth to run down to Mrs Robinson, explain what had happened and ask if she would look after the smaller children while she and George looked after Rebecca and Martha drove them all in the sulky to the Doctor in Beverley.

In spite of their past differences, Edith immediately snatched up a bottle of brandy and ran up to the rectory where Martha, accepting her advice, worked some of the stimulant into Rebecca's mouth.

The journey into Beverley was something that Martha could never recall. George and Elizabeth held Rebecca gently between them all the way. By the time they reached the doctor's house it was apparent that the little girl was dangerously ill. Her breathing was shallow and she was running a temperature and passing blood.

The doctor considered sending her on the evening train to York but decided she was too ill to move. He explained to Martha that he would keep her at his house where his wife could assist him observe Rebecca until the morning. If she were better then he would put her with Martha on the train to York. Arrangements were made by the railway telegraph to alert the York hospital to this plan.

Dr Watson's wife put Rebecca to bed and showed Martha a room at the back of the house where she could sleep. Martha meanwhile sent Elizabeth and George home in the sulky with instructions to drive into York the day after next, when she hoped Rebecca would be sufficiently recovered to allow her to return home.

As it was, Martha and the doctor's wife had not long settled Rebecca down for the night and Mrs Watson was sitting at her bedside when the little girl stopped breathing.

Martha was in a deep sleep when she was called and it took her some time to fully comprehend that her daughter was dead.

Understandably she completely forgot her instruction to George to go to York with the sulky to pick her up and it was not until she saw him driving in at the gate to the doctor's house just before noon that she remembered.

"How did you know to come here, George?" His mother asked as she stood bareheaded in the sun beside the sulky and looked up at the boy sitting on the driver's seat, the reins in his hands.

"Peter Sievright had been into town and heard about Rebecca. Aunt Dora came up this morning and told me. I hope I did right. I brought some clothes that Aunt Dora picked out in case you wished to bury Rebecca here in town, Mum."

"Thank you dear, that was thoughtful, but I think we should take her back to Bolumbygine and bury her near her father."

"Right, Mum." The lad looked at her, blinking back his tears. "What do you want me to do now?"

She looked at him gratefully then walked to the front of the horse and held the mare's head. "Get down George and we'll take Fairy around to the back where we can leave the sulky, while we make the arrangements."

So it was that the next morning George stood with his mother and Elizabeth by the graveside in the churchyard when Rebecca was laid to rest beside her father.

Depression laid heavily on Martha and her small family for the rest of that week. It was perhaps because of her unhappiness at this time that she agreed to George's request not to be sent back to Mr Harper's school at the end of August but to be allowed to work at Broughton Park, where the Webbs were willing to take him on as a jackeroo and to teach him something of the management a farm. While George did not earn enough to make a contribution to the family it was one less to feed, which was important when money was so short.

Martha and her little family staggered through the rest of the year. At one point she was almost ready to give up when the manager of the bank in York wrote to her to advise that he had received a draft addressed to her for one hundred pounds and had credited it to her account. Martha wrote back to enquire who had sent it, as she had in mind the possibility that her father could have had a change of heart and was trying to help her.

It was some time before the bank manager replied and when he did, it was to advise that the money had been paid in cash to the Bank of Adelaide in South Australia, for transfer to her account with the West Australian Bank, York.

As Martha had no connection with anyone in South Australia, there was nothing she could do about this, except to add their anonymous benefactor to the list of people the children and she remembered in their prayers at night, a list which included Arthur Trevylian and Bill Pederick among many others.

Life continued to be dominated by the seasons and the work on the farm and it was towards the end of 1909 that Martha realised with some surprise that Elizabeth would be leaving the Beverley school at the end of the year when she turned fourteen. She was aware that the remainder of the money that had originally been collected by the parishioners for the children's education was still held in trust by the bishop. She therefore resolved to go down to Perth and apply to him to make funds available to send Elizabeth to the Sisters of the Church, who had in 1901 founded the first Church of England boarding school in West Australia.

Martha set off by train in November and was fortunate enough to make an appointment to see the bishop, who was at the time deeply involved in efforts to expand the number of church schools and also the proposed West Australian University.

The bishop remembered vividly his previous meeting with the Reverend Robert Gladwell's determined widow. He also recalled that this had led to his agreement to sell her the rectory and land at Bolumbygine. He was a man who appreciated people with strength of character and she had little difficulty in obtaining his agreement, once he had realised that she was not asking for a subsidy from church funds but only the release of money already held in trust for her children's education. The fact that the widow was also, as he described her later to his secretary, a deuced pretty little woman, was not exactly detrimental to the decision either.

Martha was delighted to have the bishop's promise and rushed off to see the sisters at their new establishment in Mount Street, where they had recently taken over a small private school from a pair of maiden ladies.

Here she ran into an apparent impasse when she was told that the places in the boarding house were all taken. The sister-in-charge indicated that while they would be happy to have Elizabeth as a student Martha would have to make arrangements for her to board with a family in Perth.

Martha had had little acquaintance with anyone in Perth since coming to West Australia. She had after all gone directly to Bolumbygine on her arrival by ship at Albany. Her brother-in-law William Gladwell's first wife Elizabeth had died shortly after her arrival in Perth and her mother-in-law Emily Gladwell had died at the end of the previous century and was buried in the East Perth Cemetery. Apart from William she had few contacts with people there and while he had recently remarried she had yet to meet his second wife.

It was while she was considering who she could possibly turn to that she thought of Charles Webb and his wife Clara, who lived at Guildford, just eight miles or so outside Perth on the railway line to Northam. She immediately returned to the boarding house in West Perth where she had been staying and collecting her valise caught the tram to William Street and walked from there to the Perth Railway Station.

Charles Webb was away from home. However, his wife

listened to Martha attentively. She asked many questions, not only about Elizabeth whom she wished to meet before finally agreeing to have her to stay, but also regarding the running of the farm. She was particularly interested with the way Martha had coped without the assistance of a husband when bringing up the children. Clara was an understanding woman who sincerely believed that most women were more capable of responding to a crisis than their menfolk. She had a deep and abiding personal regard for Martha Gladwell and by the time the latter departed to catch the late train from Guildford station to Beverley, Clara had made up her mind to have Elizabeth and to help Martha in any way she could in the future.

****

CHAPTER 14
1911

Martha looked over the bowed heads of her boys as they sat around the kitchen table. "Whose turn is it to say grace?" she asked.

"For health and strength and daily food we praise thy name. Oh Lord. Amen." Piped nine-year-old Timothy at high speed then reached out his hand to the crusty hot bread roll on the top of the heaped plate in the middle of the table.

Schwack, went the little riding crop that Martha kept hooked by its leather thong on the back of her chair at meal times. However, Tim, who was her favourite after Elizabeth, had anticipated her reaction and withdrawn his hand.

With a hurt look he raised his dark brown eyes innocently to his mother and enquired in a polite voice, "Would you care for me to pass you the rolls, Mama? There is a lovely crusty one on the top that I thought you would enjoy."

Anthony, aged fourteen, looked at his elder brother Douglas and nudged him.

Martha ladled wheatmeal porridge from the black iron saucepan into a bowl and addressed her eldest son. "George, would you care for porridge?"

George looked up. He had been dreaming as usual: "Err...yes, please Mama."

Martha addressed the others in turn and served up the wheatmeal.

There was silence except for the sounds of healthy young boys eating.

"Did you see Elizabeth when you were over at Broughton yesterday?" Martha asked George, when, initial hunger blunted, he began breaking a roll into pieces and spreading them with honey.

"No, Mama," he replied. "I asked Mrs Webb whether she was around and she said that Elizabeth was out, shepherding some sheep along the river."

"What a shame. I wonder whether she plans to come home this weekend."

Martha was pleased that Elizabeth was so happy with the Webbs and approved of her doing whatever she could to help, but was disappointed that she had not come home to see her now that it was school holiday time. After all, Elizabeth would be leaving school in December and would need to obtain employment of some sort.

Douglas was a boarder at Mr Harper's school that had been taken over by the Church of England and was now called Guildford Grammar School. There he made up part of the cost of his keep by serving as a monitor and helping supervise the younger boys' homework in the evenings and on Saturdays. Douglas was an excellent scholar and the headmaster was already talking of him going on to the new University that the Bishop and other prominent citizens had made such efforts to establish in Perth.

Her brother-in-law had written to advise that funds had come to hand from his father's estate for the education of her children. While there was not a large sum available there would be enough to provide for the education of one of the boys at the Grammar school for three years commencing early in the New Year. Anthony's future education would therefore be assured.

She became aware that Douglas was talking to her. "I am sorry dear, I'm afraid I was wool gathering and far away. What is it you said?"

"That I heard Mathew and Mark Robinson say that the Webb's have to sell another block of land. We adjoin it they said, on the north side of Pederick's paddock."

"I am sorry if that is the case," she replied. "Mr Webb has been a friend to us these many years. It will be sad if he has to sell any more of the land he inherited."

"Mark says it is because Harry Webb has been spending all their money, building a rabbit netting boundary fence right around Broughton. Mr Robinson said they should have concentrated on clearing land and fence it later, when it was producing."

"It has nothing to do with fences. Mr Sievright says that it is because Charlotte Webb is always buying clothes and Harry Webb wastes money on fast women and slow racehorses." Anthony cried in an excited torrent of words.

The little riding crop flicked the incautious youngster on his wrist.

"Anthony, how dare you! You know very well that you mustn't speak of such things, especially in front of a lady," his mother admonished him.

"Sorry, Mama," he said apologetically as he ruefully rubbed his arm. "But Mrs Webb does spend a lot of money, you have said so yourself. Just think of that motor that she drove up here from Perth last year."

"Did you see it, Anthony?" piped Tim, all eyes, from the other side of the table.

"No, but I bet I'll see motors every day when I am at the Grammar School with Douglas." Anthony replied grandly.

A few days later a letter arrived from the Sisters of the Church. In it they suggested that Elizabeth, whom they described as a brilliant student, should stay on at Perth College for another year and then go to the University.

Martha worried a great deal about this and eventually wrote back to explain that there were insufficient funds available to support Elizabeth for another year as she still had to ensure that the remaining child Tim, had his chance to go to a private school too.

Almost immediately the sisters replied, offering to waive the normal school fees if it were possible for Martha to arrange to board her privately for a further year. They also asked if, in return, Martha would be willing for Elizabeth to accept the responsibility of a monitor and assist with the running of the Lady Margaret School, their small annexe for young children at Guildford.

Martha decided that, before replying, she would drive over to Broughton Park where Elizabeth was staying with Clara Webb to see the latter and to discuss this possible arrangement with them both.

Leaving Tim in the care of Douglas, she took Anthony with her and drove off in the surrey. As she climbed the hill on the far side of her land she passed Charles Webb and his son Harry talking to two young men wearing riding breeches and boots. Charles lifted his hat as she passed and she waved. Harry Webb said something to the young men and they laughed.

As she drove up to the big house at Broughton she noticed a large motor car was parked under the trees, its brass lamps gleaming in the sunlight.

"Hello Martha," said Charlotte coming on to the verandah. "What do you think of the Lejeune boys' motor car? It's a Rolls and they brought it with them by steamer from Calcutta. It looks magnificent doesn't it and quite puts my De Dion to shade."

"I don't know very much about motors, Charlotte," Martha acknowledged. "They seem to be much more trouble than a horse to manage and are always breaking down or getting a puncture."

"Ah, but the speed at which they travel! We made the trip from Guildford to York in two hours the other day and were out here having picked up the mail and some stores in less than an hour and a half. Three and a half-hours from Guildford travelling comfortably. It's a new age you know." She smiled at her friend.

Martha eyed her, expensively attired in a smart green morning dress, then asked her where her mother-in-law was.

Charlotte answered her casually, "Oh, somewhere around." Leaning against the verandah post she added pensively, "I rather like the look of the Lejeunes, Martha. Father Webb is very taken with them too. The younger brother has been very sick with cholera and is only just out of convalescence. Perhaps, if they buy that block from us," she mused, "I'll come up here more often."

Martha frowned and asked after Charlotte's children, who were much the same age as her own.

Charlotte looked at her and laughed gaily, and then led the way into the house where they found Mrs Webb writing at a pretty bonheur de jour style desk.

"Oh, Martha," Clara cried, "just the person I wanted to see. I am glad that you have come over, as otherwise I was going to ask Charlotte to drive me to Bolumbygine in the sulky. You'll want to see Elizabeth; the dear girl is outside helping the cook make up a list of stores we need from town. Charlotte will you please tell her that Martha is here."

"No, please don't tell her I am here just yet. There is something I want to discuss with you, Mrs Webb."

Martha accepted Clara's invitation to sit down and explained the reason for her visit, showing her the letters she had received from the Sisters at Elizabeth's school.

"This is wonderful, Martha," said Clara, looking up from the letter she was reading. "You must give Elizabeth every encouragement to take up this opportunity. Don't you worry, she can continue to stay with us at Guildford. I always enjoy her company and if you wish it, she can live with me when it is time for her to go on to the University."

Martha thanked her gratefully and went with Charlotte to find her daughter.

When they found her, Elizabeth was in animated conversation with a young man sitting on a table at the far end of the storeroom, where he carelessly swung his legs. Elizabeth knelt on the floor before the shelves, a notebook and pencil in her hands.

She does look pretty, Martha thought, her dark hair caught up by that red ribbon, her oval face lightly tanned from hours spent riding, now flushed as she riposted to a remark from Charlotte's son Tom.

"Hello, Mrs Gladwell," Tom called, springing off the table with a clash of spurs as he caught sight of her. "I had better be off or Grandfather will be giving me a lecture about wasting time again. Goodbye Mrs Gladwell, have you come to take Elizabeth home for a while?" Not waiting for a reply he went on, "Please tell George that I'll drop over to see him and the boys one day."

Aha! thought Martha, so that's the way the wind blows. Well, Elizabeth and Tom have known each other for many years, long before Elizabeth had gone to live with Clara. Aloud, she explained the purpose of her visit and that Mrs Webb had offered to let Elizabeth continue to stay with her while she was at school and perhaps when she was at University too, if she finally decided to go there.

Elizabeth was excited by the prospect and though she had already discussed the possibility of going to the University with the Sisters, this latest confirmation of the proposal moved her to tears.

The Lejeunes purchased the block adjoining Martha's land from the Webbs and quickly set up camp on a hillside overlooking the valley and close to the springs. They called their newly acquired property Myuna, which was the aboriginal word for good drinking water. They rapidly set about developing the property, felling the trees and burning the stumps out of the ground with the wood they had felled. The raspberry jam trees and the salmon gums burned readily enough, but they found it harder to clear the york gums where these occurred. They bought fencing wire and, having cut posts from the jam trees, drilled holes through them with a brace and bit, and ran six wires through at predetermined levels to form an effective barrier to enclose the grazing sheep.

Hard working and friendly, they were quickly accepted by their neighbours. How well they were accepted was brought home to Martha, when returning from York late one afternoon in her sulky, she saw two horses tied to a tree just off the track inside the Myuna boundary. There was a flash of white petticoat as a tall figure in a blue dress, with unmistakable red hair dodged behind a large tree. As though I wouldn't recognise your horse, Charlotte, or Robert's black mare, you really are becoming careless.

Charlotte turned up before the end of the week, carrying a letter from Elizabeth which she said she had brought from Guildford the previous day.

"It is so nice to see you, Martha," she cried, as riding side-saddle, she came to the gate. "It's lovely in the Dale at this time of year. I couldn't wait to get out of Perth."

Martha looked at her quizzically, one eyebrow raised, and said nothing.

Charlotte stared at her defiantly, then threw back her head and laughed. "I could never put anything over you, could I?" She ran her hand over her beautifully groomed hair. "Don't be disapproving Martha. I am not in the mood to be reprimanded. I ask you, what else could anyone married to Harry do, in self defence?"

She grinned ruefully and with a wave turned her horse and cantered away.

What else! Martha thought, accepting her big hearted friend as she was. A vision of her father frowning rose before her. Yes, she thought, you would think that I have let my standards slip a little. But only a little. I am just more tolerant of the behaviour of others, that is all.

The Lejeunes were not wild even though they both rapidly

became involved in all the sport that was on offer in the district. They had excellent horses that they entered in local race meetings and were soon accepted in spite of their English accents which, though initially the source of amusement, were much admired by the matrons of the district.

As soon as it was learned, and the news spread within hours, that their father was a baronet, they were besieged by invitations from every mother with pretensions to consequence and an unmarried daughter of sixteen or more. While behaving impeccably in public it would, in the Lejeunes' view, have been more than flesh and blood could stand not to sample the wares on offer. However they were both extremely shrewd and managed to escape the lures laid for them.

Martha correctly assessed their intentions as being typical of the young men of their age and class and was happy that though they were friendly neighbours, the members of her family were not subject to their influence. She was more concerned with Elizabeth's involvement with Tom Webb, Charlotte's eldest son, who had much of his mother's charm, but she wisely kept her worries to herself and in this she was comforted by Elizabeth's undoubted dedication to her studies at the university.

****

CHAPTER 15
January 1914

Elizabeth, aged nineteen, strode down the tree lined road in Guildford and turned in at the front gate, pausing to unfasten the latch on the post box to see if there had been any letters in the afternoon delivery. She found three and put one addressed to herself into her reticule. Stepping lightly onto the wooden boards of the verandah she opened the screen door and passed into the cool interior of the old house.

"Coo-ee," she called, lifting the note at the end of the bush call in the traditional manner of Australian bushmen.

"Coo-ee!" answered Clara Webb from somewhere deep inside the single story house. "Is that you Elizabeth?"

"Yes, I'll be out in a minute," Elizabeth responded and turning into her bedroom put her reticule down. She pulled off her wide straw hat and ran a comb through her thick hair. Picking up the mail, she carried it to the trellis-enclosed verandah at the rear of the house.

"Here you are, Granny Webb. It is all for you," she said to the old lady sitting on the cane lounge, her feet up, her knitting and her latest novel to hand.

Elizabeth bent and kissed the cool dry face of the woman who had become a second mother to her these last nearly five years.

The older woman looked at her steadily and marvelled at the metamorphis that had occurred to the shy little scrap of a child who had originally come to her and had blossomed first to a lovely long legged girl and now into a poised and coolly confident young woman.

She was well aware of her grandson's interest in Elizabeth, but sometimes wondered whether he was capable of appreciating the finer points of her character or whether he would turn out to be as weak as his father. Harry had always avoided the realities of life and seemed incapable of handling his strong willed wife.

"Did you find what you were looking for in the library, Elizabeth?" Clara enquired.

Elizabeth sat down, automatically keeping her knees together as she had been taught, neither her mother nor Mrs Webb approving of women who crossed their legs.

"I was lucky. I saw Mr Gault as I was leaving the library. When I told him that I couldn't find either of the books that he had set for extra reading he very kindly offered to lend me both. So I went with him to his office and collected them."

"Well, that is good, so you will have everything that you need when you go up to stay with your mother tomorrow."

"I am worried about leaving you here. I do hope that you will be all right while I am away."

"My dear, it is far too hot for me at Broughton at this time of year. I would have liked your mother to have come down to stay, but you know only too well that she will not leave her home summer or winter. I really do wonder sometimes whether she is ever going to leave the management of the farm to your brother George."

"He has the working of the farm now, but mother is always worried he won't have enough to eat if she's not there to cook for him." Elizabeth smiled at the old lady, then changed the subject. "I saw Douglas today. He was in the medical section of the library. He told me that he had received very good marks in all his subjects last term and that he now has every hope of being accepted at Adelaide for second year medicine."

The old woman nodded and looked at her over her spectacles. "That is good isn't it; your mother will be pleased." She smiled encouragingly.

The young girl looked at her worriedly, "I don't know. It was one thing for him to do first year in Perth, where he was able to work part time at the Grammar School, but what is he going to do for money in Adelaide? He says that he will have saved enough for the first term before he leaves here."

"I am sorry that things are so bad at Broughton just now and that we are not able to do more to assist him. It has been a bad year for us all including your mother, poor dear. Mr Webb is finding that the farm barely provides a living. Can't that man who befriended you all those years ago, help now? What was his name? I forget, though he is often in the newspaper these days with his mining interests and his transport business."

"Oh, you mean Arthur Trevylian. Mother gets very upset if anyone even suggests she should write to him for help, though I am sure he would be delighted to do so. You know he sent money at one time anonymously to Uncle William, to pay for Anthony and then Tim to go to the Grammar School. Uncle William pretended that it was a legacy from Grandfather Gladwell's estate, but eventually mother found out from Uncle William's wife and she was furious. It was a long time before she calmed down."

"He has been very kind to you and has no family of his own. I wonder sometimes whether your mother isn't wrong not to accept the help he offers."

"I don't know, I always wondered whether he had been keen on mother at some time and that she had refused him. I can remember him quite well when he was staying with us just before Rebecca died. I also remember his fairheaded friend Bill Pederick."

"I don't know what happened, Elizabeth. Your mother is very private and never confided in me. She was a very pretty woman in those days. It would have been difficult for her to remarry at that time. Few men would have wanted to take on six children."

The older woman looked pensively out into the garden where the sunlight was fast fading.

In spite of the heat, Martha experienced a real lift to her spirits the first week that Elizabeth was home. The young people with their fun and laughter made her forget for a while her financial troubles and suddenly the house was crowded with the sons and daughters of her neighbours coming and going.

Broughton Park had a tennis court to one side of the house that was in constant use that summer. Built of clay that Charles Webb had had carted in from the salt lakes to the east of Beverley, the surface was fast and hard, yet required a minimum of maintenance except to touch up the lines with lime wash from time to time.

The Lejeune brothers were regulars on Sunday mornings, playing with Charlotte and whichever of her sons, Tom, Des or Charlie were available. George Gladwell didn't play tennis and in any case preferred to spend his time with the Sievright boys. Elizabeth did play and her younger brothers, Anthony and Tim, were often invited on a Saturday afternoon when Vicky and Sally Webb would join them in a game.

The day following Elizabeth's return to Bolumbygine, Tom Webb had ridden over to the rectory with an invitation from Charlotte to Martha and the youngsters to tea and tennis at Broughton on the next Saturday.

When they arrived in the sulky, Charlotte met them and suggested that the two young Gladwell boys should play a set with Vicky and Sally before tea was served. Tom, she said, would be in later, to partner Elizabeth against Martha and Charlie the youngest of her boys who was the best tennis player of them all.

Martha declined saying that she would prefer to sit in the shade and it was finally decided that Charlotte herself should partner her youngest son.

Vicky spun her racket to determine who should play with whom and she and Anthony settled down to a brisk game with Sally and Tim, while the others seated themselves in cane chairs on the verandah to watch.

By the time tea was brought out to the verandah and the players came up to enjoy sandwiches and sponge cake, the set had been played out to a tie.

After a housemaid had removed the tea things, the other players went on to the court while Sally took Tim off to see her new pony in the paddock on the other side of the creek.

Vicky and Anthony sat on the verandah until, finding the game boring, Vicky suggested that Anthony come and see her mother's new saddle at the stables.

Martha, only half listening, nodded agreement and, with her feet on a cane stool, watched the game in progress.

The game became a battle royal and the best part of an hour passed before Charlotte declared that she was too puffed to continue and conceded the set to Elizabeth and Tom.

Reaching the cool of the verandah she chatted to Martha then looked around her. She saw Sally and Tim sitting and talking on the other side of the garden, and asked Martha where Vicky and Anthony were.

Martha looked at her in surprise. "Oh! Now where did Vicky say they were going? I know, she said they were going to the stables to look at a new saddle you had bought, Charlotte. They went off to the stables a few minutes ago."

Charlotte frowned and having given instructions to the maid to bring more lemonade excused herself and went off to look for her elder daughter.

When Vicky had suggested that they should go and see her mother's saddle at the stables Anthony had been inclined to to remain where they were. But Vicky had nodded meaningfully to him and scowled. Intrigued, he had agreed and followed her around the side of the house. When they reached the saddle room Vicky led him straight past the door and into the chaff room where she threw herself onto some bags of chaff and leaned back against the heap stacked almost up to the roof.

"Come and sit down, Anthony," she commanded, patting the bag beside her. "Don't be frightened, I am not going to eat you."

He sat beside her awkwardly, leaned back on the next bag, and looked at his pretty companion. Lying back on the chaff, her blonde hair held back by a blue ribbon, she surveyed him through narrowed eyes.

"Don't you get bored when you are up here?" she asked casually.

"Not really," he answered candidly. "I enjoy it more than school."

She flounced. "Well, I find it a bore. I much prefer the city rather than the country." She looked down at her feet, then up at him out of the corner of her eyes. "The men up here are so naïve; they have no experience."

Anthony gasped! He sat up with a jerk and looked away, then turning back to her enquired. "What do you mean, no experience?"

"Experience with women, I mean. They're just country boys," she added languidly, then laughed. "Most of them know about the birds and bees, after all they could hardly avoid that, what with rams and bulls and the things that go on around a farm. The problem is that they can't learn all they should know from watching the farm animals, especially about how a man makes love to a girl properly or what she wants from him to please her."

Anthony's eyes opened in wonder. He had never heard a girl talk like this in his life. "Well, of course," he croaked. He was developing a lump in his throat. "Most important thing, er… to understand what a woman needs."

"I don't think you have any idea what I'm talking about Anthony. I think you would run a mile from a real woman."

Anthony looked at her in horror, his eyes widening as he stared at her.

"What do you mean?" he stammered.

She laughed derisively. "There, that's what I mean. Country boys are so naïve; you have to explain everything. You are like the rest and have no ideas of your own."

Anthony looked at the door anxiously, desperately afraid that someone would come looking for them and hear what she was saying.

Vickie saw the panic in his eyes and decided to go for the kill. "Come here and I'll teach you how to kiss me," and she reached for him.

Charlotte walked rapidly up the slight rise in the direction of the stables.

She was worried at Vicky's prolonged absence with Anthony and concerned she would find the two together. Charlotte was intent on maintaining her daughter's reputation, as she knew only too well that her own and Harry's behaviour had been such that any slight infringement of the social mores would be frowned upon and would react to the detriment of the family generally if it became common knowledge.

Panting a little from the climb she stopped short of the building and called, "Vicky, Anthony, where are you?"

Repeating this she circled the stable, careful to keep facing outwards across the horse paddock as though expecting them to appear from the far side.

Vicky heard her mother's voice and pushing Anthony aside sat up and shook her skirt down.

"What's wrong, Vicky?" asked Anthony, his face flushed with excitement.

"Mother's come up here to look for us." She buttoned the front of her blouse and taking the ribbon out of her hair retied it. " You had better do up your trousers and straighten yourself. Don't worry, she won't come looking for us in here; she's too frightened of what she may find and what the neighbours will think if there is a fuss."

Anthony gaped at her matter of fact attitude to possible discovery, but in response to her further urging stood up, tucked his shirt inside his trousers and made himself as tidy as possible.

For the remainder of the time Elisabeth and Anthony were at home, Tom Webb was a regular visitor at the Rectory, while Anthony would often take a horse and ride up the track towards Broughton. There, he told his mother, he was studying a large colony of galahs, watching the pink and grey parrots coming and going in the trees on the edge of the steep hillside above the Lejeunes block.

Tom Webb on the other hand seemed quite content to sit on the verandah with Elizabeth and Martha, holding skeins of wool while Elizabeth wound them into balls for Martha's knitting as they talked.

Martha was pleased to encourage Tom's visits, for she knew Elizabeth enjoyed his company, in any case he was her favourite among the younger Webbs. She felt that Elizabeth of all her children was the most level-headed and that nothing more would come of it, at least until after she graduated at the end of the year.

****

CHAPTER 16
August 1914

Martha took long walks in the bush in the cooler months, usually with Dora Sievright, who had an abiding interest in the forest trees and especially the wild flowers that abounded in spring. For many years the two women had been making a collection of dried wildflowers, a hobby that they found both interesting and satisfying.

Spring was earlier than usual, when, in pursuit of this innocent occupation they each took a small cane basket and set out along the river. Walking past the mudbrick house that the Lejeune boys had built set back from the road, they followed the top of the riverbank looking for wild orchids.

They walked slowly several yards apart, searching amongst the fresh growth for the frail plants with their delicate spiky flowers, when Martha stumbled and heard the rustle of an animal they had disturbed. She stopped and, head up, listening, heard the rustle again below her. Looking towards the river she saw Charlotte and Robert Lejeune lying together on a rug spread out on a canvas ground sheet, a second rug thrown over them. She stood transfixed as Charlotte propped herself up on her elbow. Smiling at Robert, she lowered her head and kissed him, then caught sight of Martha watching her, hands held to her face.

Charlotte's happy look changed to one of disbelief and then dawning fury.

"What's the matter, Charlie?" asked Robert, his voice thick with emotion. "Give me another kiss to remember you by. I have to return home to England tomorrow."

Charlotte, deliberately lowered her eyes and embraced her lover.

Martha, her face crimson with embarrassment, turned and

stole away. When she was out of sight of the couple below, she ran to Dora.

"Martha, Martha slow down. Whatever is wrong? You look as though you have seen a ghost," Dora asked anxiously. Martha looked at her wildly for a moment, then without a word she sat down on a fallen log and stared at the ground in front of her, her basket clasped in her hands.

Martha's face had been flushed and was now chalk white. Wisely Dora let her recover her composure.

"I had a funny turn. I was walking along and I stumbled on... something. It caught me by surprise, that's all," she said haltingly. She was not a good liar and her words came in bursts as she tried to think of what to say without Dora realising what she had seen. Finding she was still tightly gripping the handle of the basket she put it down and lowered her face into her hands.

Dora said nothing. She stepped forward and picking up her friend's basket, gripped Martha's small hand and pulled her upright.

"Let's go home. I won't ask you any more questions. You have obviously given yourself a fright. I've often done that," she laughed. "I looked up in our bedroom the other night and saw a shadow on the wall that I took to be a man in the lamplight. It turned out to be nothing, a curtain moving in the wind."

They walked silently back the way they had come, both deep in their own thoughts.

I can hardly tell Martha that I had seen the horses tied to the tree and Charlotte and Robert Lejeune on the ground. Poor Martha, she has always liked Charlotte and has been the first to take her part. It must have been a terrible shock to find that her friend has feet of clay. But then should I judge Charlotte? I've always had the feeling that Harry Webb was unfaithful to her and surely one could hardly blame her if she strayed too. The Lord knows, it cannot be easy for someone as affectionate and outgoing as she is. Ugh! Dora shuddered; it would be horrible to be married to a man like Harry. I am so grateful that I married Fred.

When they reached the rectory, Edith Robinson met them.

"Have you heard the news?" she gasped at them, distraught.

Martha stopped short, her eyes wary as she regarded the unrepentant gossip.

Dora set her basket on the edge of the verandah and sat down heavily beside it. Squinting into the midday sun, she looked up at Edith. "Spit it out."

"Mathew was in town with Luke and John last night and they heard that the German army has marched into Belgium. England and France are going to help Belgium and our government has called for volunteers for the army," Edith said in a low voice, her face puckered with emotion, her eyes full of tears.

Dora looked serious. "That is terrible, but it is nothing to be upset about, Edith," she said in her practical way. "It is a long way from here and the French have a huge army, strongest in the world I read somewhere."

Edith burst into sobs, crying with the racking gasps of an old woman, tears streaming down her cheeks. The other women looked at each other.

"Better put the kettle on, Martha," Dora said, "we're going to need a nice strong cup of tea."

"You don't understand," moaned Edith. "You just don't understand."

Martha crossed the verandah, heading for the kitchen, then stopped.

"You just don't understand," Edith repeated herself, "John and Luke have gone to Perth, to the barracks in Francis Street to join up. Oh! Oh! I'll never see them again, they'll go to the war and be killed, I know they will."

Dora stood up and put her arm around the smaller woman to comfort her.

"Now Edith, it's probably not as bad as it seems. They will have to pass a medical, like the men had to when the Light Horse went to the Boer War. After all the medical problems they have had over the years, Luke's flat feet and the growing pains in John's legs that used to keep him awake and you sleepless at night, they'll be rejected for sure."

Edith turned her face towards Dora as she leaned on her shoulder, "Do you really think so Dora? They're so young."

Martha, thinking of Edith's boys, doubted whether anybody could reject such healthy young animals even though, now she thought about it, she realised that they were not as young as they used to be. She turned and, opening the kitchen door, went in.

The next afternoon there was a knock on the back door of the rectory. Going to it, Martha saw Charlotte standing there in her best green riding costume.

Remembering the circumstances of their last meeting, Martha was apprehensive, then realised that Charlotte looked strained and had dark circles under her eyes.

"Whatever's wrong, Charlotte?" Martha asked kindly. Even as she spoke, she thought, heaven's not Harry, or the boys.

Charlotte looked at her. "I couldn't sleep last night. I thought you would be the only one who would understand, so I came here, as soon as I had said goodbye to him."

"Goodbye to whom?" Martha was having difficulty following the direction the conversation was taking.

"Robert, of course." Charlotte snapped out the words, then shrugging her shoulders, she relaxed, then sagged, one hand against the wall. "May I come in Martha and sit down, please?"

Martha recovered herself and apologised. Inviting Charlotte into the kitchen, she told her to sit down at the table and to tell her exactly what had happened.

Martha moved to the stove, lifted the hotplate, centred the kettle over the small flame and turning around, stood with her back to the stove.

"Has Robert been recalled to his regiment?" she enquired.

"Robert had a letter three months ago from someone in London saying that they thought war was inevitable. Almost by the next boat, his old Colonel wrote offering him a place in the regiment, to which he replied that he would consider the offer and let them know. When he heard the way things were developing, he sent off a wire last week to the P & O Company's agent in Fremantle asking for information regarding their sailings for next month. However, the news the night before last decided him. He left this morning to catch the train from York and called in at the house on his way. I hardly had a minute alone with him. The boys were there, staring at him as if he was.... Oh God! Martha I'll never see him again, I know I won't." Charlotte put her head down and started to cry.

Martha said nothing, just moved closer and putting her arm around her friend, held her to her side.

"I knew it couldn't last," Charlotte said. "The difference in our ages was too great. While he was here, I was ready to do anything, anything I tell you, to keep him."

"I know how you felt Charlotte, I can truly understand how it is."

"It wasn't enough. He said that he had to go. He was like an old war-horse. He said that he felt that the other chaps would be going without him and that he had to go. Oh! Oh, Martha, why did they have to start fighting? Why is it always the women who have to stay behind?"

"I don't know Charlotte. What about his brother, John, will he have to go too? They have only just got that farm going. Someone will have to look after it."

"John is going to stay here to take off the crop, Robert said. Then he plans to go to England and join up, but Robert thinks the war will be over by Christmas. His worry was that it would be over before ever he got there." Her voice rose and she turned a tear stained face towards Martha. "Men are such fools; spoiled little boys with honey on their faces, always looking for more."

****

CHAPTER 17
Lemnos, Greece. April 1915

Corporal Desmond Webb of the Australian Imperial Forces looked at the extraordinary scene in Mudros harbour. More than two hundred vessels of all sorts were crowded here, warships and merchant ships; even ferryboats and pleasure steamers from the Clyde had been pressed into service to carry the troops. The big battleships and cruisers were moored in long lines down the length of the harbour with destroyers and submarines in clumps along the sides. There was a constant coming and going of motor boats and ship's pinnaces, and the smoke haze from hundreds of funnels hung over the scene. On the ship nearest him troops were exercising in preparation for the coming assault, with rope ladders to get down into the boats moored alongside. He casually watched the men swarming back out of the boats and up the side of the vessel.

Below him there was a sudden shout of laughter. He turned and, leaning over the forecastle rail of the elderly ship, looked at the crowded deck below. There were half naked soldiers everywhere, lying on the deck and the sheeted hatch covers, or sitting in little groups playing cards.

Directly below him a pair of sergeants running a game of two-up stood on the hatch cover with a crowd of men below them on the deck. A man from time to time sprang on to the canvas-covered boards of the hatch cover. Picking up the kip he took his turn, betting against men in the crowd below that the two coins he threw high into the air would drop with either two heads or two tails upward when they landed on the hatch.

Des watched for a while then turned to the young man lying on the deck beside him reading, his service cap propped over his eyes, his body burned as dark as any Arab and his swarthy face completing the illusion of a Levantine origin.

"George, George Gladwell," Des called, to the younger man. "Can you lend me a couple of quid until pay day?"

"What happened to the last pound you borrowed from your brother?"

Des grinned and pushed back the lock of red hair that had fallen over his eyes. "Lost it playing poker last night. I couldn't ask Tom for another advance just now, he'd be too disapproving."

George turned his head and surveyed him casually, his dark eyes expressionless. "You really are an idiot, aren't you. Don't you ever know when to stop?"

"No," said Des cheerfully. "I need to borrow some money to help me beat the boredom of lying around on this tub. Bloody hell, we've been here nearly three weeks. I thought Alex was the pits, but this is worse."

George pondered this comment as he remained on his back then, hearing another roar of laughter from the two-up game below, he came to a decision.

"I am not going to lend you any more money," he said decisively. "I'm going to offer you a share in a business partnership. We'll go down and play together. You take the kip, I'll put up the cash while it lasts and we'll share the winnings. But on the clear understanding that we stop when I say so. Agreed?"

Des looked at his friend as though he had gone mad then laughed. "Sure, I agree. I've nothing to lose," he stopped, then said uneasily, "but you never gamble, George. You could lose your money, you know."

George grinned at him. "I thought that is what you wanted me to do? Come on." He stood up and, tucking his book under his arm, led the way to the crowd around the hatch.

The sergeant presiding over the game stepped to the edge of the hatch cover in the expectant hush and looked down at the two coins where they lay almost side by side.

"I'll be buggered!" he exclaimed, half to himself. Then he called: "Tails it is!"

There was a groan from the front row of men, followed by cheers from the rear, "Good Old Webby! Good on yer mate!"

The sergeant picked up the coins and went over to where Des was standing, with George beside him. The other man held the stakes, his foot on a roll of notes.

The sergeant spoke to George. "Well, what are you going to do? That's twenty times in a row and I've never seen anyone do that before?"

Des said quickly, "What about it George, we've won over fifteen hundred quid? Better give it a miss!"

George regarded Des dispassionately; he was sweating profusely, whether due to the warmth of the April sun or excitement, he didn't know. He felt quite detached. After all he had put his initial stake money away the moment they had won the first two tosses and he felt he had nothing to lose. Des looked at him almost pleadingly as though he was willing George to stop.

George turned back to the sergeant and smiled. "No," he said, "we can't take it with us, so let's give it another go."

"All up again?" croaked the sergeant, who was starting to find the tension more than he could take.

"All up. Tails." George said firmly, indicating he was betting all their winnings on the single toss of the coins.

The sergeants appealed to the crowd to cover the bet but finding they were short, appealed to the men coming up to join the crowd to have a bet.

"Come on you lucky lads, these boys have called tails twenty times in a row. The odds of tails turning up again are a million to one, so what have you to lose."

"Lend us a quid, Jack and I'll be in it," cried one.

The sergeant shook his head. "I'm not that stupid," he said ruefully.

At last they covered all of George's money and the sergeant nodded to Des to toss.

A hush came over the ship as Des moved into the centre of the hatch. He laid the two pennies out on the kip, a short piece of well used board about four inches long, a quarter thick and an inch and a half wide that he held horizontal in his right hand, his first and second fingers under it to support it. The coins were placed one in front of the other on top. Looking carefully about him to ensure there was enough clear space, he took a deep breath and tossed the coins high into the air with a sharp twist of his wrist.

The well-polished coins glinted in the sunlight as they spun in the air, then fell with a double clink onto the hard canvas stretched tight over the hatch cover.

The crowd swayed as the men strained to see how they lay and the sergeant paced deliberately forward and bent to look at the upwards face of the coins.

"Tails it is," he cried.

There was a deathly silence, then pandemonium as the soldiers who had not bet roared with laugher at the discomfiture of those who had.

George turned to the sergeant who was holding the stakes and put out his hand.

"I'll take that lot now, thank you," he said quietly. Removing the bundle of money from the dazed man's fingers, George started to count out his winnings.

Satisfied, he turned to Des, who was standing in a dream in the middle of the hatch cover and, signalling him to follow, jumped off the hatch onto the deck.

It was a clear night, the stars still shining even though there was light on the eastern horizon. Sitting packed into the bow of the ship's lifeboat George could see little except the heads of the men around him. The dull thud of the steam engine in the pinnace towing them stopped and one of the seamen on the thwart behind climbed over the patient soldiers and loosed the towline from the bow.

The Australians had been brought from Lemnos by three British battleships. The fifteen hundred men who were to make the initial assault had been assembled on deck in the dark and given a last hot drink before going over the side into the ship's boats. Packed in tightly, with their heavy packs, they had been towed towards the coast first by the big ships and then, when they were a mile or so offshore, by naval steam pinnaces.

Smoking and talking had been forbidden and there was nothing to do except to look at the dark line of hills ahead, etched by the glow to the south east of the Turkish searchlights as they ranged the sky in the Narrows on the other side of the peninsula.

A low voiced order was given at the stern and the seamen unshipped their oars and, in response to a further order, quietly gave way. George, who had become used to the easy motion of the boat dozed off, as the oarsmen settled down to the creaking pull to the shore.

"Jesus! Just look at that!"

The low exclamation caused a stir amongst the men and looking forward George saw a rocket shoot up from the cliff above and exploding, cast the weird light of a magnesium flare across the sea.

Rifle fire broke out from the point on the south side.

The men started to move, gathering their rifles.

"Sit down," a sharp voice ordered from the bow where the young subaltern who was to lead them ashore was now standing. Timber Wood, a young farmer from Bruce Rock, had joined the battalion before George and was popular with the men.

They were almost at the beach now and George could see the low waves creaming in to break on the sand.

"Ship oars!"

The seamen shipped their oars and the boat glided onward, to ground heavily. Two men jumped over the bow and, standing chest deep in the water, held the boat.

Suddenly they were all standing. George felt the weight of his pack bearing down on his shoulders and hefted the rifle in his hand. The lieutenant was on the beach now, a revolver in his hand, the sergeant beside him. The men scrambled forward to get ashore.

The boat rocked as the weight shifted throwing several men in a heap. George staggered as a heavy body pushed past him.

"Bloody hell! Wilkinson, watch where you're going," he cried as he fought to regain his feet.

The other man growled something in reply and pushing through from behind him, thrust George aside. He paused, standing on the gunwhale just back from the bow and leaping into the black water with his rifle and heavy pack, disappeared from view.

George looked at the place the man had gone down with horror.

"Get on Gladwell, we haven't got all day," snarled a voice behind him. Looking up to find nobody in front of him, George stepped to the bow and onto the gunwhale. Then jumping forward, he found his footing on the firm sand of the bottom and struggled ashore without mishap.

They had been told to expect level ground and good going for the first few hundred yards the other side of the beach, but what he saw was a steep slope covered with low scrub rearing above them across a narrow strip of sand.

There had been more fire from above and a machine gun opened up, tracers arcing over their heads. Two men, the sergeant and the lieutenant, were lying in a crumpled heap at the water's edge; George was surprised to see them so still.

Stumbling ashore he had seen the men were forming themselves into a rough line facing along the beach. Further along the little bay small figures were running down the slope and onto the sand. Enemy, he wondered?

He had seen few men hit though he had heard their cries and as he looked around him he saw that he was close to Des

Webb, who had discarded his pack and was standing, his rife held in front of him.

"Fix bayonets," an authoritative voice called and he heard the rasp of metal as the short swords were withdrawn from the scabbards and a series of metallic clicks as they locked, the sound lost in a renewed burst of fire from above.

"Imshi Yallah, piss off, you lot," Des shouted. He charged forward yelling like a dervish and, taking up the cry, the men surged after him.

Caught up in the excitement of the moment like the others, George ran after Des, crazily shouting "Imshi, Imshi Allah."

There was pandemonium as the Australian troops, released from their enforced inaction in the boats, surged along the beach towards the small group of Turks, their rifles held before them, bayonets glinting in the growing light.

The Turks had arrived on the sand in a mob. They looked at the screaming tide of men pouring along the beach towards them and, dropping their rifles, turned and ran off up the hill again with Des, George and two or three others at their heels.

Clutching at roots and boulders as he hauled himself up Des led the way, ignoring those Turks who, winded, had fallen aside. Just below the crest, when blown and short of wind, he realised the others had dropped out of the scrambling race, Des turned into a gully that appeared to provide a path to the hill top on their right. Pulling themselves up over the ground, tearing at the stunted growth, he and George finally came to the top of the slope, where they threw themselves gasping on the ground.

Recovered, they raised their heads and looking around, found themselves alone.

The Turkish fire from their side of the bay had stopped and there was only desultory rifle fire from the headland of Gaba Tepe further to their right. Below them they could hear shouted commands to the men on the beach and scrambling sounds as the troops poured after them up the narrow path.

A big miner from Kalgoorlie, Walker by name, had followed them up the slope. Like George he was still carrying his pack. Des stood up and turned to them and waved them enthusiastically onward.

"No, wait 'ere mate," called Walker. "They told us to stick together, not to go 'areing all over the shot, like a blue arsed fly."

Des turned back. "George," he said, ignoring Walker, "you leave your pack here with Walker, just bring your water bottle and your rifle. We'll follow up these jokers and keep them moving now they've started to run."

Without waiting for George to reply he turned and set off again across the bare ground towards the first of the tumbled ridges of Chunuk Bair.

"Won't be long, Walker." George said and sliding out of the straps of his pack, he picked up his rifle and ran after Des.

There was no organised defence ahead and no firing above the beach. The only Turkish soldiers they could see were a small group of men filing up a path over the shoulder of the Sari Bair range that forms the spine of the Gallipoli peninsula.

Des set a cracking pace after the Turks, outrunning the other parties of Australians as he picked his way across through the patches of low scrub towards the hills above.

Within two hours they reached the crest of the range where, lying on their stomachs, they had a panoramic view across to the Narrows. Behind them to the west there was more gunfire including the occasional crack of a field gun. Closer to the right they could see a small detachment of Australians winding down from the ridge. Immediately below, a larger body of Turkish infantry in extended formation was probing forward towards the Australian patrol.

Des spoke quietly. "George, we had better do something to warn our blokes that the Turks are in front of them. Let's get into the shade of that big rock, where we're not silhouetted against the sky."

He wriggled back off the crest then led the way forward

again to where the rock he had mentioned provided a natural strong point. Below them the Turks had taken up position in a shallow gully and were lying with their bayonets fixed, waiting for the small party of Australians to come up to them.

"George, pick one of the Turks and take aim, remembering to make allowance for the plunging shot. I'll do the same and then when I give the word, fire one round. That will alert our fellows. The smoke will blow away before the Turks can turn to look for us."

They both took careful aim and fired together. There was a faint puff of dust among the men, who promptly hugged the ground.

They lay quietly as the sound of scattered firing came from below. Des waited until it was quiet, then raising his head peered through a small bush.

"They're still there and our lot have gone to ground. It looks as though they've got the message."

They stayed where they were, taking the occasional brief look to ensure they could follow what was happening. Neither side was moving.

At last Des asked. "This is thirsty work, have you any water?"

"Yes, some, but where is yours?" George was concerned as the sun already had some heat in it.

"Left it behind with my pack. I didn't expect we would be away so long." Des grinned, embarrassed.

George stared at him in amazement. "Well, of all the idiots you'd take the ticket. You can't stay out in this heat without water. You had better go back and tell the first officer you meet that there is nothing much between this point and the coast. If they move quickly we could get right across to the Narrows and cut the peninsula off."

Des hesitated, then understanding the logic of George's thinking agreed he would return to the beach. "All right, you stay here. I'll go and get reinforcements."

He crawled to the side of the rock and when he had the rock between himself and the Turks stood up. Lifting his hand in farewell he turned towards the way they had come. As he did so, there was a dull thump like someone beating a bundle of rags with a stick. Des's legs folded and he fell forward first onto his knees and then his face.

George felt sick with surprise as he saw it happen, and gazed dully at the body of his friend lying beside the rock.

Coming to his senses, he looked to his left to see if he could identify the source of the shot. There was nothing and in any case he realised that he hadn't heard the shot.

"Are you all right, Des?" he called, but there was no answer. With rising anxiety he lay there trying to quarter the ground to see if there were any Turks on that side. Apart from the troops below him who were finally moving off, there was nothing to be seen. He crawled over to Des who was lying on his stomach, unconscious and breathing heavily through his mouth. He looked very young and vulnerable, his face white under its tan. George looked him over carefully and could see no sign of blood. Briefly he felt relieved, then realised that it didn't mean anything. Kneeling beside him, George turned Des onto his back, undid the clasp of his webbing belt and unbuttoned his uniform. With difficulty he removed the uniform coat and pulled up his shirt. There was no sign of injury. Turning him over, he saw a small round hole beside the lower spine from which blood was slowly seeping. It looked such a very small wound, but perhaps the bullet had damaged the spine. Quickly he pulled a field dressing from his pocket and, placing it over the wound, secured it as best he could.

Des lay unmoving while George pondered the situation. There was nothing for it but to try to get him back to a casualty clearing station, he decided. Placing his own rifle against a small bush where he could pick it up easily, he hid Des's Lee-Enfield amongst the rocks and pulled some scrub over it.

George looked around him carefully. There was no sign of

Turkish troops in the valley or the Australians. He grasped Des under his arms and, lifting him, managed to shrug the limp body over one shoulder. Bending his knees with difficulty he picked up the rifle and set off back the way they had come.

It was a nightmare, carrying the weight of his friend in the heat, not daring to put him down in case he was unable to summon the strength to lift him again. Being short of water, George was in a state of near collapse by the time he reached the Australian outposts.

There was a brisk firefight going on at the time on the southern side of the beachhead, but coming in through the broken ground from the north he was able to walk amongst the Australians before any one noticed him.

George was staggering with fatigue, his head down, when he heard the crunch of boots and a welcome voice.

"'ere! Bear up mate! Let's 'ave 'im."

George saw a pair of khaki clad legs in front of him, then hands lifted Des from his shoulder and laid him on the ground. Relieved of his burden, he staggered backwards and sank to the ground where he lay to rest his aching back and closed his eyes.

"Stretcher bearers!" cried a voice nearby. The call was passed on by other voices into the distance.

George became aware of other boots crunching towards him.

"What's the matter with this man, Corporal?" asked a broad accented voice.

"Dunno, sir. He came up that gully there, carrying this bloke. He's just about buggered."

"What about the other man? Is he wounded?"

" Yes, sir. He's been shot in the back. He's out for the count, sir."

George struggled to sit up and seeing an officer with a thick greying moustache, looked up to him questioningly.

"I know who you are," said the grey haired officer. "You're

George Gladwell from Bolumbygine. My name's Pederick; do you remember me?"

"Yes, sir." George could see now that the man wore the crown of a major on his shoulders and made to get up.

"Stay where you are man. Just get your breath back while we send your mate off to the field aid post. Then you can tell me where you two have come from."

George watched as Des was lifted on to a stretcher and taken away.

Major Pederick sat down and taking out a handkerchief wiped his forehead.

"Well, young George," he said. "What have you been up to?"

George explained what had happened and that there were very few enemy troops to be seen between the Sadi Bair Range and The Narrows.

Pederick seemed amazed but having questioned George closely he wrote out a message and, calling for a runner, sent it off to his battalion commander.

Then he stood and shook hands with George. "Well done young fellah, you haven't changed! I expect you will want to find your own lot now. Last time I heard, they were down there on the right of the line." He pointed away in the distance. "Like me to send someone with you to show you the way?"

George had almost entirely recovered by now. "No thank you, sir." he said briskly. "I'm all right now. I'll find my own way across to them."

"Right then, I'll say good bye. Good luck to you." Major Pederick turned away.

Things were becoming organised and when George arrived back at the hill above the beach, he found that down below there was already a casualty clearing station set up to tend to the wounded before they were shipped off in small boats out to the ships standing off shore. Looking down at the lines of stretchers waiting for the boats he wondered which one was Des.

He found his pack where he had left it at the top of the gully then set off to the south to look for his unit. He found it with the rest of the battalion, where they were busily engaged in fighting off a Turkish counter attack that had driven them back almost to the beach. It was a long hard day, the fighting confused, and he was lucky to be among men he knew. From what they told him most of the men had started off as though they were playing a game with the Turks, in and out of the narrow gullies that seemed to cross the area in all directions. However it had quickly been borne upon them that their mates were getting killed and, as the first excitement evaporated, they had realised the benefit of cover and had taken to moving in a slower, more deliberate, fashion.

The worst aspect had been the shortage of water and George believed that it had been this fact alone that had held them back. That the Turks had made a number of almost suicidal attacks on the Australian positions had not really registered with him. Like many of the young men with him, he had only a narrow view of what was going on and was only glad to be alive as he scratched tiredly at the hard rocky ground that night trying to dig in with the wholly inadequate entrenching tool he carried.

As it was, it was the need to find cover and water to stay alive that became the overriding concern, not only that first night but during the succeeding days they remained hemmed in among the hills.

****

CHAPTER 18
May 1915

Martha adjusted her hat and, picking up the basket that contained the liniment for Ted Robinson's shoulder, walked out of the kitchen leaving the door on the latch. As she reached the garden gate she noticed the geraniums against the fence in the shade of the pepper tree were jaded and looked up at the late afternoon sky. Not a cloud, she thought, and it is already the third week in May. Well, they do say that the season will be all right provided it rains before Empire Day and that's 24th of May. The day after would have been Rebecca's sixteenth birthday, had she lived.

She stood head down, thinking of the happy little girl she had lost, then straightening her shoulders, set off along the track towards the Robinson's.

Looking to the right she saw young Tim by the shed doing something to the stump jump plough Arthur had given them. A born farmer, she thought, already at thirteen more capable of handling big working horses than his father ever was. He'll be checking that the machines are ready to put in the crop just as soon as the opening rains come. He's leaving Beverley school at the end of the year. I wonder whether I was wise to agree that he should come home on the farm and not go to the Grammar School?

A large magpie swooped down from the trees and with a thrashing of wings passed close over her head, making her duck. "Go away, you horrid bird," she shouted, and picking up a stick waved it around over her head as a second magpie launched itself from a dead tree behind her. At least it is a good sign that they are nesting this early, she thought. George always liked the hoarse cries of the magpies. He used to stand on the verandah and listen to them and to the butcherbirds in the early morning. I wonder where he is this morning. I do hope he is safe.

Poor Charlotte. Elizabeth had written from Guildford that a telegram had come for Charlotte to say that Des Webb had died of wounds on the Greek Island of Lemnos, having been with his battalion when it landed on the Gallipoli Peninsula on the 25th of April. Then she had received George's cheerful letter dated 23rd March, when he said he was with Tom and Des Webb who were both fit, though they were bored stiff and their feet sore from too much marching. Martha could only surmise that George and Tom were on Gallipoli, and just hoped they were alive.

Every family in the district seemed to have young men with the Australian forces. The younger Robinson boys, Luke and John, together with Peter Sievright, were with the 10th Light horse. John Lejeune, who instead of going to England to join a British regiment, had elected to join as a private soldier in the AIF and was now serving as a Captain with the 28th Battalion.

As Martha turned into the gate at the back of the Robinson's she looked up to see Edith's face at the kitchen window.

Edith had never bothered much with a flower garden, but she always made sure that everything was neat and tidy. There were no leaves on the ground or a thing out of place on the verandah.

The screen door swung open and Edith's usually raucous voice sounded muted as she hailed Martha. "Well, look what the wind has blown in."

Martha looked around her, "No sign of any break in the wind drought we're having, Edith. Tim spent three hours on the top of our mill yesterday turning the wheel by hand to pump some water for the sheep. We're used to a wind drought in April, but not for this long. It's halfway through May now."

Stepping on to the verandah, she walked briskly towards the older woman. "How are you Edith? I've brought you some liniment for Ted's shoulder; it has always been a sovereign remedy for muscular troubles."

"Thank you for that kind thought Martha. The trouble is that he gets so stiff in his shoulder and neck he can hardly move some mornings. He shouldn't work so hard, but with Luke and John away in the army there is too much to do here, especially now that Mark is spending so much of his time helping the blacksmith in Beverley." Edith frowned, but didn't elaborate further on the reason Mark had left the farm.

Martha said nothing, knowing that Mark had never seen eye to eye with his elder brother. After all, the farm would be hard pressed to provide for them all now that Mathew, who was over forty, was getting married to a much younger girl from the other side of York. If the war goes on young women may find there is a shortage of men of any age to marry, she mused. It wasn't like that a few years ago, when every incoming ship to Albany or Fremantle was crowded with unmarried men coming to look for instant wealth on the Goldfields. Men of all ages had far outnumbered women then. No wonder the Government and the police had licensed properly run houses in Kalgoorlie and other towns on the Goldfields for women who catered for the men's baser needs.

She realised that Edith had been talking to her and that she had mentioned Luke's name. "Sorry Edith," she said. "I had a sudden thought."

"I said that Luke has been ill with fever in hospital in Malta, we've had a letter that Mathew brought in last night." Edith said quietly. "At least while he is there he is not at the front with the rest of the boys."

"Yes, that is true. It's terrible that we should be thankful that one of our sons has fever if that means he is out of the front line. I just wish the censorship was not so strict and that I knew where George is."

George at that moment was sitting in a hole on the hill slope above Anzac Cove, the warmth of the morning sun soaking into his half-naked body, his slouch hat shading his eyes. He looked at the sparkling blue water and thought how different it was from the black oily sea they had crossed when they had landed four weeks ago. Today, naked men bathed in the warm water as they relaxed before returning to the dust, heat, and stench of the battlefield above. As he watched the swimmers a shell came over the headland and burst, showering the sea further out in the bay with shrapnel. Laughter and abuse wafted up to him from the men in the water. Other men lying under the shade of blankets or ground sheets in their holes on the hill slope cursed the Turkish gunners, then turned on their side and went back to sleep.

George took out a cigarette, struck a match and lit up. Reclining at his ease in his hole he drew slowly on the Woodbine then closed his eyes as he wondered what they would be doing on the farm. He tried to picture in his mind's eye the land sloping down from the rectory to the little church and to forget that tonight he had to go back to the stinking hell of the trenches above.

The war continued and for some months there were no further casualties among the men from Bolumbygine. Then out of the blue had come a telegram to the Robinson's advising them that Luke was dead. Edith was shattered. She had had a number of letters from Luke in which he had told her that he was recovering slowly from fever and as a result she was quite unprepared for his death.

Martha and Dora both did their best to comfort her but she was inconsolable and for a time they all wondered whether she would lose her reason. However it was the news that Peter Sievright had been seriously wounded that finally jerked Edith out of herself.

For some reason the official telegram had gone astray and

the first Dora knew about it was when she picked up their mail at the Beverley Post Office.

The sight of Peter's letter had lifted Dora's spirits as she made her way out of the building to where Fred waited in their buggy outside the store.

"Got the mail I see," he grunted, eyeing the brown envelope on top, which he recognised as being the poor quality of the writing materials available to the troops.

"Yes, a letter from Peter. Would you like me to read it to you now?" She enquired looking at him.

"No, not now. Let's have it after tea when we have time to think about it."

As a result it was not until well after dark that Dora finally took the small bundle of letters from the kitchen dresser and started going through the ritual of reading them to Fred. She kept the letter from Peter to last.

"It is not his handwriting, Fred," she said as she opened it. As she scanned it she became still, finally raising her eyes to him from an ashen face. "It is written for him by a nurse from the Island of Lemnos. He's aboard a hospital ship in the port of Mudros. He has been wounded in the head, but is much better now and making good progress. What does that mean Fred, good progress from what? What happened?"

Fred sat in his chair, sucking his pipe quietly, more disconcerted than he could express. "Poor old Pete, wounded in the head. Doesn't sound too good does it?"

She pushed the letter over to him. "Here you read it, I can't, not out loud." She sat upright in the chair, lost in her thoughts.

Fred read the letter slowly, his pipe on the table beside him, blue smoke curling upward from its bowl.

"It seems he was hit by shrapnel and that he lost an eye. Well, at least the other one is still good. He says that the doctors think they will be able to patch his face together given time and he may be sent to Egypt to recover in the base hospital there. When was this written?" He turned the letter over. "Eighth of

September. Mmm! He says he was wounded on the seventh of August so that means he must be over the worst of it, Dora."

He read on. "He says that he has seen most of the Bolumbygine boys. George Gladwell, he says, was in the initial landing and came through scot-free. He was sorry to hear about Des Webb but doesn't mention Luke Robinson, so perhaps he doesn't know that Luke is dead too." He looked at her. "Well Dora, he sounds cheerful enough and the nurse says in a note at the bottom that he will be able to write himself once he gets the bandage off his hand. What do you make of it all?"

Dora was sitting, her shoulders slumped, crying quietly.

Fred stood up and reached across the table. "Hold hard, old girl," he said awkwardly, "don't go on so. He's not dead. He's been knocked about a bit but it could be worse you know."

She lifted her head and looked at him witheringly. "Knocked about a bit! He's lost an eye, he's wounded in the head, he can't write because of his hand, it's not healed and he was wounded a month ago. Knocked about a bit!" her voice rose. "It's obvious that he has been terribly hurt and I wasn't there to help him. He shouldn't have gone in the first place, all this talk about loyalty to the old country. That's all right in peacetime, but these boys are being killed and maimed. Who is going to look after our Peter in the future if he can't work on the farm? Not those politicians who took us into the war."

"Now then, hold hard Dora. It is not my fault you know. We were both proud of him, proud of the way he went straight off in the first lot to join up. I suppose the problem is that we never thought he could be hurt like this."

Dora was depressed for days and after she had received more letters from Alexandria telling her of Peter's continued recovery, she was still deeply worried as to his future. There was nothing that Fred or for that matter Martha could do to help her adjust to the situation. In spite of her long enmity to

Edith Robinson, it was Edith with whom she was able to relax and to talk of her fears. After all Edith had lost Luke and seemed to understand.

At Broughton Park, where Elizabeth was now living with old Mrs Webb, they were finding the shortage of labour a major problem. In addition to her duties as secretary and housekeeper to Clara Webb and her husband Charles, Elizabeth had now taken on the work of stockman. As a result she was in the saddle almost daily, either riding the fences to ensure they were in good order or shepherding the sheep along the river while keeping an eye open for ewes that were having trouble lambing.

She loved the work in the open air, but Mrs Webb was worried about her, especially because of what she called the waste of Elizabeth's efforts at the University to obtain her degree.

Charlotte had in some way reached a balance in her relationship with her husband Harry, who was back and involved full time in the management of the property now that their manager had left and was with the 28th Battalion in Egypt.

Life, Clara said, had not been so free of tantrums and the unhappiness of constant quarrels in years. That is until her youngest grandson Charlie announced that he too was leaving to join the army. The whole family jumped on him as one. Elizabeth, a bystander, was horrified at the behaviour of people whom she had known so long.

Charlotte wept, shouted and screamed by turns, declaring that her last son was not going. Harry Webb, for once in his life, was clearly disturbed at the prospect of losing the assistance of his youngest son. How could he be expected to run the property with only the help of old men and young girls, he complained to anyone who would listen. He freely admitted that Elizabeth knew what she was doing with stock but Vicky or Sally had not shown the slightest interest in the farm or anything else, other than men.

Charlie argued that at twenty-one he was certainly not the youngest man to join the Australian army. The more his mother raged and everyone else tried to persuade him to change his mind, the more adamant was his resolve to join the AIF. He was of age and didn't require his father's permission to join the army and he would go, he said. And he did, riding his horse into York early one morning and leaving it in the town pound for his father to collect at his leisure.

After Charlie's departure, the big house returned to something close to normal, though only the usual stock work and essential maintenance to buildings and fences on the farm was carried out. Everything else had to wait for better times.

****

Chapter 19

They'll never come again

The fawn coloured tide of sheep moved slowly through the scrub along the river bank, first one and then another darting forward to eat the fresh leaves that had shot from the base of the jam trees and the small gum saplings. An old ewe, realising her lamb was no longer with her, broke off her quest for food and in a frenzy of contrition ran around calling for it. At last she recognised the lamb's response from the bed of the river and stopped and stamped her forefeet. The sheep ceased feeding and turned their heads then, recognising a mother's warning to her lamb, returned to their grazing.

A jingle of harness disturbed the scene as the horse standing under a white gum shook its head to rid it of the flies around its nose. The young woman sitting on its back, reading, her leg casually hooked across the pommel of the saddle, looked up and cast her eye over the sheep, to make sure they were all feeding into the wind and none had doubled back.

Elizabeth returned to reading the letter from Tom Webb that she had received the day before. It was the love letter of a man who had survived three years of war. Having left most of his friends and a brother at Gallipoli in 1915, Tom had been thrown into the hell of Flanders the following year, only to see the raw recruits that had joined them on Salisbury Plain mown down, first at Fleubaix and then Poziers. His letters were full of plans for the future, when he would breed merinos with plain bodies more suited to being shorn with modern machines than the wrinkled skin that Bonooke had made fashionable in the past.

His letters arrived spasmodically due to the combination of his own periods in the trenches when he was not always able to get them into the hands of the Army Postal Units, and the delays caused by the limited shipping to Australia.

Elizabeth was aware that Clara Webb approved of her correspondence with Tom and understood that they planned to marry once he came home. Charlotte on the other hand was not a good correspondent and greatly resented the letters Elizabeth received from Tom. This had led to more than one unfortunate display of temper on Charlotte's part, when Elizabeth had felt the contents too personal to share with Tom's mother.

At the rectory, Elizabeth's mother was still managing the farm with the help of Tim. Even though times were difficult, they had been fortunate in the seasons since 1914 and the crops had been good. The return from these plus the advance paid on wool that had been acquired by the government had provided them with a living, though there was little surplus that Martha could send to Douglas, now in second year at medical school in Adelaide.

Elizabeth sent him money when she could, which was little enough, as the Webbs were wholly dependent on wool from Broughton for their income and existed on loans secured against future proceeds when the wool could be freely sold.

Anthony on the other hand had been more fortunate as Arthur Trevylian, now a successful man with widespread commercial interests, had set up a trust fund through Cowan, Dibney and West to provide for him while he was studying law in Perth.

The sun was lowering in the sky when Elizabeth, calling the dog out from under the acacia beside her, started to move the sheep out of the river and back towards the homestead where she would put them into one of the fenced paddocks for the night.

By the time she had unsaddled the horse and let it go in the horse paddock it was almost dark. Turning towards the house she saw that the oil lamps had been lit in the kitchen. She crossed the verandah and was headed towards the outside stair to the floor above when Clara Webb called to her from the kitchen door.

"Elizabeth, don't be too long. We are going to have an early dinner tonight as Mr Webb and Harry will be driving in to town to a lodge meeting."

"Very well Mrs Webb. Do you think that Mr Webb would mind dropping a note for mother into the rectory as he goes past?"

"I am sure he wouldn't mind dropping it in for you, if it's ready now."

"Thank you, I'll bring it down when I come." Elizabeth clattered up the stairs to her room, to wash and change her clothes.

When they were all sitting at the long wax polished jarrah table in the dining room and Elizabeth had helped the cook bring in the meal she realised that Charlotte, as often was the case, was not present.

"Would you mind dropping a note off to my mother at the rectory as you go past, Mr Webb?" Elizabeth asked the old gentleman. "There's a kerosene tin she uses for a letter box on the post beside the road, so you wouldn't have to actually turn in to the house."

The old man lifted his head and looked at her. "Certainly my dear, I'll be delighted to be your messenger," he smiled at her, then continued carving the roast leg of mutton.

"Where's Charlotte got to this time, Clara?" Charles Webb asked his wife as he sat down to his dinner.

"I don't know, I am sure. She said that she was going riding and put on that green habit of hers, the one she wears when she is going to Bolumbygine, but she didn't say."

Harry looked across the table at Elizabeth and shrugged his shoulders. "You never know with Charlotte, so it's no good surmising. She'll be back before long. I thought I heard a horse coming up the road as I was coming down to dinner. But I haven't heard her moving about upstairs and could be mistaken."

Elizabeth said nothing, even though she had seen the red

tinged hair of her employers' daughter-in-law glint in the light of the kitchen door as Charlotte had flitted across the verandah and up the back stairs just before they had rung the bell for dinner.

As it was they had almost finished their first course when Charlotte, very neat in a white blouse and a dark blue skirt, came into the dining room and slipped into her place.

"I am sorry that I am late, Papa," she said to Charles Webb at the head of the table. Turning to Clara added "I brought back two small plants for you, Mama, that Mrs Sievright sent. She struck them for you from cuttings taken from her red bougainvillaea."

"Oh, is that where you've been?" Mrs Webb looked surprised.

Charlotte looked across the table at Elizabeth. "Yes," she smiled. "I went to see Martha and found her out. So I went on to the Sievrights on the off chance and found her there with Dora and Edith Robinson, who by the way is looking very old and tired these days. We had a cup of tea and then the younger Sievright boy, Peter, came in. He's very shy of visitors, or so I gather, but Martha persuaded him to join us and I must say Edith is a changed woman. She spoke so kindly to him and they all carried on without any fuss whatsoever, even when he dropped his cup. He is still very weak in that hand, you know."

Charles Webb passed Elizabeth a plate with a serving of meat on it, to which she added vegetables from the side board before placing it before Charlotte.

"Was Peter Sievright very badly wounded?" he asked kindly.

Charlotte thanked Elizabeth, then replied to the question. "Yes, he was, Papa."

She paused and looked across at the weak face of her husband staring at her, then turning to her father-in-law she declared harshly. "Peter was never good looking but the effect of the injury when he lost his eye has been to draw his eyelid down on one side. The doctors have tried to patch his face together on that side, but the surgery has left him with a long puckered scar across his forehead and up into his hairline. He now has a glass eye which helps to give him some appearance of normality, but the surgeons will never be able to do anything to rectify the disfigurement on that side. The other side of his face is perfectly normal and if you look at him from that side you would never know he had been wounded. Mind you, Peter is quite matter of fact about it all and said he is fortunate to be home, though Dora says that he is often in pain and his arm may never be fully functional again."

Clara Webb spoke quietly from the end of the table. "I have no doubt Dora Sievright is only too glad to have him home, however he is."

"That's true. I felt that Edith and I were in agreement that, whereas Dora had finally come to terms with the situation, we would not have coped as well."

Harry Webb rose to his feet and looked down at his wife with something close to distaste. "For God's sake, Charlotte!" he cried, "do you have to be so morbid? None of these boys had to go; they went to get away from this place. If I had been younger I would have joined them!"

Charlotte looked at him scornfully. "What utter rubbish you do talk Harry. All you want to do is to swan around in Perth. You're fed up because you are having to do some real work for a change."

Harry turned white at this charge and leaned towards her menacingly.

"At least I do some work, which is more than you do. You're upset because the Lejeunes have gone and you have nobody to run after. Perhaps you'll try your wiles on Peter Sievright; that would be about your level," he sneered.

Charlotte flushed to the roots of her hair and leaned forward in her chair towards him, her face contorted with fury.

"You bastard!" she spat the words at him. "You know that

you are worse than useless as a husband with your funny little games. I despise you!"

Charles Webb was on his feet by this time.

"Silence!" he thundered. "How dare either of you behave like this in front of my wife and Elizabeth, a young girl. Harry, you will apologise to Charlotte and your mother immediately, then leave the room. Go and get ready to go into Beverley."

Harry started to say something to his father, but dropped his eyes before the old man's fierce stare. He mumbled an apology to Charlotte and his mother then left the room.

Charlotte looked wildly about her, then she too pushed her chair back and left the room, her head erect and back straight as she walked through the door into the hall.

The front door opened and closed and there was silence in the room.

"Would you care for some pudding, Elizabeth?" Clara Webb asked quietly from the end of the table.

It was about an hour and a half later that the dogs started to bark. Charlotte, pleading the onset of a migraine, had made her excuses and gone to bed immediately Harry and his father left for Beverley.

Elizabeth was in the kitchen making a hot drink for Clara Webb when the latter called out. "Elizabeth, someone is at the back door. Will you go and see who it is, please?"

Picking up the oil lamp Elizabeth opened the kitchen door and stepped on to the verandah where she saw the figure of a man at the door into the hall.

"It's only me, Elizabeth. Peter Sievright."

"Oh, hello Peter! I haven't seen you for a long time, please come in."

He came towards her then stopped and pulling two small envelopes from the breast pocket of his shirt, held them out to her.

"No, I won't if you don't mind. Dad and Fred went into

town and they picked up the mail. There were a lot of telegrams for people around the district and they brought those for Bolumbygine home. There were two for Mr and Mrs Harry Webb and one each for your mother and the Robinsons. Mum thought I should bring these over straight away, while she and Dad went up to see your mother and then the Robinsons."

She looked down at the yellowish coloured envelopes, recognising them for what they were, she was afraid to take them from him. Hesitantly, she looked at him again, her fear showing in her eyes.

"Oh, Peter! What has happened, there must have been the most terrible battle somewhere?" she gasped.

"Yes, but George is alive. He was wounded on the third of May and is in hospital in England. I couldn't catch my horse immediately and by the time I had saddled up and was riding this way, Mum and Dad were already walking down to the Robinsons and they told me that your mum was so relieved. Anyway, here are the telegrams." He held them out to her again.

Elizabeth put out her hand and took the envelopes, not daring to think of their contents.

"Young Mrs Webb is in bed asleep, but you had better come in Peter, and see Mrs Webb. She is in the sitting room" Elizabeth beckoned to him.

"No, Elizabeth, I won't if you don't mind," he said gently. "It's my face, you see. It'll upset her at this time. I'll be off home."

He turned and limped stiffly off the verandah into the darkness.

Elizabeth looked after him, grateful for his thoughtfulness. Closing the screen door she added an extra cup and saucer to the tray for Charlotte and carried the tray into the sitting room.

"Who was that Elizabeth? Why didn't you bring him in?" The old lady demanded, looking over the top of her reading glasses.

"It was Peter Sievright. His father had picked up some mail for Mr Harry and thought it was urgent enough to send straight over."

"Mail? They don't usually pick up our mail." Clara Webb enquired testily.

"There were a number of telegrams, including one each to my mother and the Robinsons, as well as the two for here. It may be bad news."

The old lady seemed to shrink into herself. "Two telegrams? Oh, Lord, not both of them." Her eyes filled as she looked at Elizabeth pleadingly.

Elizabeth knelt and putting her arms around the old lady spontaneously, she held her for a while. Sitting back on her heels, she said earnestly. "I must go and tell young Mrs Webb. I don't think she is in bed as I heard her moving around upstairs."

The old lady shook herself and gathering her resolve spoke briskly. "Yes, you must do that. Please go and tell her I want to see her down here."

Charlotte came down dressed in a gown of her favourite green, her hair immaculately brushed as always, cascading over her shoulders.

Elizabeth had told her that the telegrams had arrived and she had had time to compose herself prior to entering the sitting room.

The old lady was sitting slumped in her chair as they entered the room, but sat up straight with an obvious effort and lifting her head looked at her daughter-in-law. "I am afraid that both boys may have been hurt, Charlotte. Perhaps you would prefer to open these envelopes in the privacy of your room." She held them out.

Charlotte took them, then seeing Elizabeth move towards the door spoke as she tore them open. "No, don't go Elizabeth. You are a member of the family and I am quite aware that you will be just as concerned as we are."

She read the contents of the first envelope in silence, her eyes narrowing, then the second and drew a deep breath. Passing both telegraph forms to Mrs Webb she looked at Elizabeth standing quietly by the table her face hopeless.

"Tom is dead." Charlotte spoke harshly. "They're both dead, killed in action on the third of May." She took a step jerkily towards the young girl. "You poor child, he'll never come home now. They'll never come…..home again." Her voice broke. "I've lost all my sons. Oh, oh, Charlie how could you?" She leaned against the mantelpiece and wept.

Elizabeth slumped quietly to the floor in a faint, where she lay in an untidy heap.

The old lady sat quite still for some time, then grunted, and heaving herself up from her chair, she went to Charlotte to comfort her.

The cries of the magpies in the gum trees outside filtered into the bedroom. To Elizabeth they sounded like querulous women standing in a churchyard gossiping after church. She lay staring at the ceiling of her bedroom, tracing with her eyes the fine plaster crack that, rising in the corner above her, meandered out into the expanse of the ceiling before diving down to meet the scotia at the joint with the wall. From where she was it looked like a blocky rectangle that was slightly out of square, the map of Western Australia, she thought.

She frowned, recalling the events of the previous evening. She remembered coming to her senses on the floor of the sitting room, the brass wheel at the curved extremity of the leg of the sofa table filling her vision as she struggled to recall what had happened. Charlotte had bent over her and called her name then helped her to her feet and half carried her upstairs. Where with Mrs Webb's assistance she had put her to bed, the smell of their perfume, Lavender Water and Eau de Cologne, had remained with her after they kissed her good night.

Elizabeth thought of Tom, a happy laughing face, serious the day he had told her of his intention to join up. She felt again the deep despondency that had overwhelmed her during the night when, awakening from a deep sleep to the still of the night, she had realised that she could hear murmuring voices along the verandah where the younger Webb's bedroom lay.

She decided again that she must put all thought of what may have been out of her mind. Tom's face had already become less real to her for she realised that he must have changed in the years he had been away and now she would never see him again.

Tears gathered in her eyes and, welling over, ran down her cheeks. She lay there feeling unhappy, sorry that she would never speak to him again, would never be able to tell him how much she had longed for him. There was so much she had planned to say to him and now would never have the opportunity to express.

A brisk step on the verandah was followed by a knock on the door. In response to her invitation Charlotte entered the room and sitting on the side of the bed looked down at her kindly. She looked tired, her eyes red rimmed, her hair as always well brushed and shining, her white shirtfront blouse crisp and freshly starched.

"I know exactly how you feel, Elizabeth, and believe me I am grateful to have someone who will understand and sympathise with me."

She leaned forward and kissed the young girl on the cheek and holding her shoulder gave it a squeeze.

"Is Mrs Webb all right? I should be up now, I am so sorry." Elizabeth struggled to sit up.

Charlotte shook her head. "There is no hurry, nobody is up yet. I've told Mrs Kennedy that we will have a late breakfast. After that I thought we should perhaps go over to Bolumbygine to see your mother. She will be worried out of her mind over your brother George. We ought to go and see poor

Mrs Robinson too. Mrs Kennedy said that one of the men from Myuna came through this morning and told her that John Robinson was wounded too and on the same day."

She stared out of the door, watching the clean limbs of the lemon scented gums moving against the clear sky.

Sighing, she stood up and said. "Yes, that's what we must do, Elizabeth. We must ride over to see your mother and Edith Robinson."

****

CHAPTER 20

The mine salting king: 1920

Anthony Gladwell came out of the building that housed the offices of Cowan Dibney and West into the glare of the sunshine in St Georges Terrace and paused to adjust his tie as he waited for his friend and colleague John Long to join him.

He tilted his straw boater slightly over his eyes and looked up and down the wide street, watching the office girls tripping along on their way to lunch. It was a hot day and many of the girls wore thin blouses through which he could see the outline of their breasts.

One or two of the girls, looking at the delicately chiselled features of the young man standing at the top of the steps, were aware of his glance.

"Surveying the quality of what's on offer, Tony?" The drawled question caused him to swing around.

"Well, why not?" he demanded of the tall young man standing beside him. "If they wanted to they could cover up rather than show themselves off to the world."

John Long glanced languidly at his friend and noted with amusement that his mouth was slack with repressed excitement. "Perhaps if you're feeling like this, I ought to take you over to the other side of the railway."

Anthony considered the suggestion, then reluctantly put the thought aside.

They started off down the street, exchanging greetings with acquaintances.

John drawled casually. "Amazing place, Perth. You can't walk down the Terrace without seeing someone you know. Stands to reason I suppose being a small country town. Not like Melbourne you know."

Anthony shot a glance at him. Yes, he thought, we have all

heard about your trip to Melbourne and your family's connections there.

Aloud he said. "No, and probably never will be, but there's plenty of money to be made here, if you don't bet on slow race horses. "

His companion winced, having lost more than he could afford on a horse he had assured Anthony was a dead certainty to win at the races the previous Saturday.

Anthony grinned maliciously and changed the subject. "I have to look at a brief for my uncle this afternoon. I don't know why he always expects me to do everything immediately and he is far more demanding than the other partners."

John didn't answer, but looked at the passing crowd as they came up to William Street and waited until the policeman directing the traffic in the centre of the street junction, signalled to them to cross.

"That's your sister, isn't it Anthony? Over there, standing outside the Palace Hotel waiting to cross in this direction. By Jove, she's a handsome girl. Why doesn't she get married. I would have thought that she would have had them down on their knees to her in droves?"

Anthony saw Elizabeth on the other side of the street at the same moment as she saw them and waved.

"Yes," he smiled and returned her greeting. " She is good looking. However, there is currently no man in her life, as far as I know. There have been many interested, but the chap she was keen on, Tom Webb, was killed in France in 1917. She has never encouraged anyone since. Certainly not after she obtained a position at the University."

John Long considered this, then said. "Oh, is that so. A blue stocking no less. Well, she would be wasted if she went through life like that."

The sound of the police whistle galvanised the crowd waiting to cross the street to action and they walked to where Elizabeth was standing.

"Hello, Elizabeth, how are you? This is John Long, you may have met before." Anthony kissed his sister on the cheek.

Elizabeth turned to the other young man and smiled. "No, I don't think we have. How do you do, Mr Long." Turning back to Anthony she said. " I am waiting for Charlotte Webb; we're going to lunch together at her club. Now that I have seen you, Anthony, I must remind you not to forget that you are coming to Ventnor Avenue to lunch on Sunday."

Anthony grinned, looking boyish. "I won't forget, not if Sally is going to be there."

A slight frown gathered on Elizabeth's brow. "She will, though I don't know whether she will be staying for lunch as I did hear her say that she was going out in the afternoon to play tennis. John Lejeune is coming to pick her up in his new car."

Anthony looked shocked, his confidence wavering. "Good Lord, surely she is not going out with Lejeune. He's old enough to be her father and in any case, wasn't he her mother's er…. friend, before the war?"

Elizabeth flushed. "Anthony! You must not repeat malicious gossip and in all truth it was John's elder brother, Robert, that the talk was about." she added in confusion. "There's Charlotte, I must be going," and with barely a nod to John Long she left them standing on the corner and dashed across the street.

"Well, you certainly upset her equilibrium," murmured John. He stood gazing after the slim figure with an amused look on his face as she half ran down the Terrace to where a tall woman, dressed in the height of fashion, was waiting.

"Elizabeth is very fond of Charlotte Webb and will never hear a word against her, even if Charlotte was a tear-away before the war." Anthony put his hand on his friend's arm. "Come on and I'll buy you a drink." and he shouldered his way through the batwing doors into the front bar of the Palace Hotel.

Lewis Saloman pursed his thick lips. He was a heavily built man of medium height who, in spite of his thickening girth, exuded energy as he sat gazing unseeingly through the window at the broad expanse of the Swan River. He took a deep breath. Swinging around in his chair towards the big desk he leaned forward and looked at William Gladwell from under thick eyebrows.

"Well, Gladwell, what do you think is the proper defence to an allegation like this? You're the lawyer, not me. I am only a simple man. It would seem to me that mister bloody Trevylian is on the wrong track in trying to help the Gold Squad bring an action against me, just because the Louisa Jane mine has not been able to go on producing ore that grades at two ounces of gold per ton for ever. Nobody could have foretold the heavily metallized area would run out just where it did." He stared with hooded eyes at the man sitting in the swivel chair on the other side of the desk.

William Gladwell did not answer immediately. He was aware that this man was one of Cowan Dibney and West's biggest clients and at the same time had few illusions as to his character. Lew Saloman had fought his way up, literally from the bottom of the pit shaft, a penniless Slovene who had found his way to the West Australian Goldfields at the turn of the century just after the mines were first opened up at Southern Cross. His only school had been the back streets of Trieste, where he had learned more about human beings and their frailties as a pimp for his mother and two sisters before he was ten years of age than the majority of men do in a lifetime.

Once on the Goldfields he had quickly grasped the fact that there was little chance of advancement as a miner working a piece of ground under the tribute system and he had joined the fledgling miner's union as an organiser and representative of the many Italians and Slavs. From that point on, due to his native intelligence and cunning as much as his readiness to use the strength of his massive shoulders and his big fists, he had risen rapidly within the infant organisation.

He had also earned well-deserved respect for his ability to negotiate. Once word had got around the Goldfields that a deal handled by Lew Saloman stayed a deal, regardless of who was a party to it, he was besieged, not only by the miners who were trying to extract a reasonable living from their toil, but also the representatives of the mine owners, who wanted to keep the mines working without stoppages due to labour disputes.

Inevitably, Saloman was given the opportunity to acquire equity in the mining companies on favourable terms and being naturally shrewd and careful, if risk averse with his own money, he rapidly built these initially small parcels of shares into substantial holdings. By the time war broke out in 1914 he was the Chairman and principal shareholder of a mining company with profits counted in hundreds of thousands of pounds. An extremely powerful man in West Australian business life it was only a relatively short step to a seat in the State's Legislative Assembly. However, in spite of his success, he had a weakness. He was unable to resist the lure of easy money.

In many cases the surface lode that had attracted the first prospectors to sink a shaft in the Eastern Goldfields of West Australia had been an isolated pocket of rich ore which, once worked out, had led to the early closure of the workings. However, the mining leases granted by the State Government in respect of these mines had not lapsed as they were not dependent on the area being worked continuously.

Gold mining had slumped during the war and in the immediate post-war period before gold prices again reached attractive levels, Saloman had bought up the leases of numerous small mines, often for a pittance.

As the gold price improved he sent experienced men around the workings to reassess their potential. In a few very rare cases, they found that reappraisal of the original workings revealed further payable deposits similar to the original lodes and these mines Saloman brought back into production.

However, these successes were not enough for Lew Saloman, who had gathered a small group of men around him who were not only loyal to his interests but were, in other respects, unscrupulous. These men he sent out to reopen abandoned mines and to go through the motions of mining them.

By the judicious blending of rich ore brought in secretly from other mines he owned, they proceeded to upgrade or salt the ore brought to the surface and thereby obtain good results from parcels sent for crushing at the State controlled batteries or crushing mills.

The evidence that the uncritical eyes of investors sought required only a relatively few twelve-gauge cartridges, from which the lead shot had been removed, to be reloaded with gold dust and a small number of small nuggets and fired into the rock face of the tunnels below ground. Several leases were sold off to the unwary by this ploy. There were no huge sums involved in the sale of the salted mines and, as it was not a costly operation, the resultant profits were often quite extraordinary, with little risk of exposure.

As Lew Saloman was apt to claim to his close associates, nobody could prove that a gold bearing ore deposit had not cut out one inch past the rock face that had contained the traces of gold. In apparent support of this argument there had in fact been one case where the new owners, persisting in their initial enthusiasm beyond the limits of the original prospectors' workings, had come upon a very significant gold deposit. This had led local journalists to chortle at Saloman's lack of business acumen in selling the lease cheaply.

There was one man who was able to throw light on the activities of Saloman's associates and that was the transport contractor Arthur Trevylian. He provided the wagons to carry the mining equipment that Saloman's men had used to reopen the workings and then transported the ore brought to the surface to the state batteries.

Saloman's weakness was that his men were lazy. Approached by the Police Inspector in charge of the Gold Squad, Arthur Trevylian realised what was going on. It hadn't taken the Inspector and Arthur long to work out that Saloman's men were only cleaning out the last of the loose material remaining in the mine when it closed and blending that with the gold rich ore they were bringing in from other mines. Trevylian could provide evidence that little if any drilling equipment or explosive had been used to produce the new ore that was, as Saloman's men excitedly announced to all willing to listen, responsible for the excellent results obtained from the new parcel crushed at the state battery. Inspection by the Mines Department confirmed that there had been no extension of the original tunnelling.

As Arthur had pointed out to the Inspector, it was significant that in so many cases all Lew Saloman's men had to do was to tap the end of the drive or shaft and gold fell out of the walls.

William Gladwell was aware of all this as Lew Saloman waited for his response. He realised that his client was fundamentally dishonest and had toyed with the idea of making this point so as to gain the upper hand. On reflection, he decided there was no need to offend such an affluent client, who could be relied on to pay the monumental fees involved in a lengthy court hearing. The only risk that he could see was the association of the partnership in a possibly sensational case and that would be no bad thing, especially as there was always the possibility that the prosecution would be unable to prove that Saloman had deliberately set about misleading intending buyers.

Aloud he said. "Mr Saloman, having heard what you have to say on the subject I have no doubt we will be able to put together a reasonable defence for you and your companies. But you must remember that no court case can ever be prejudged as open and shut. A case may be lost for no other reason than the judge is dyspeptic," he smiled thinly. "However, I would like to introduce you to a very clever young colleague who is already proving something of a coming star in litigation. He is in fact my deceased brother's son, Anthony Gladwell, and I would like him to handle all the research and the detailed examination of the evidence that is required to properly arm us in a case of this nature." William looked across at his client who was staring past him from his chair the other side of the desk, and waited.

Saloman sat looking into the middle distance as he wondered why William Gladwell wished to bring a younger man on to the case; not that he didn't believe in using young men when the going was tough. After all he had been at his peak himself as a young man when his brain had seemed as quick as a whiplash.

Coming to a decision he nodded his assent. "Yes, but I would like to meet your nephew first before I agree to this, Gladwell. If he is as good as you say he is he may be precisely what we require. I am of course presuming that you, yourself, will actually handle the case and that you will supervise this young man's work."

William coughed depreciatingly. "Of course, I will be supervising him. We would never allow your work to be handled by anyone except one of the partners, but in this case I am anticipating that we will be required to engage in a great deal of research and I will have need of an assistant." He reached behind him and tugged the bell pull, then turned back to his client as his secretary knocked at the door and came in.

" Miss Warren, would you ask Mr Anthony to come in for a few minutes to meet Mr Saloman please," he said.

The young woman was aware of Saloman's eyes running over her body and felt a flush start to rise up her neck. "Certainly, Mr Gladwell. He has an important client with him just now. Should he come in immediately?" she lifted her voice enquiringly.

"Tell him to come in just the same. This is a very important matter. You may ask the client if he would just mind being interrupted for a moment as we have a special point of law to put to Mr Gladwell that he may be able to help us with. Then offer the client some tea."

"Very well, Mr Gladwell," the girl breathed, blushing to the roots of her hair as she withdrew in confusion, followed by Saloman's gaze.

"Nice little chick, Gladwell," Saloman mused genially. "You fellows always do yourselves well when it comes to having a bit of fluff around."

William was not sure whether to be outraged or pleased, but decided little would be lost by agreeing with his client. "Hmp, yes, we are almost knocked down by the rush from parents of good class girls looking to find a position in professional chambers these days. There have been many changes since the war, you know. That is one of old Sir George Warren's granddaughters of course, as you would know."

There was a knock on the door and in response to William's invitation Anthony Gladwell entered and was introduced. William lost no time in explaining to the young man the reason he had been brought into the meeting. Anthony listened quietly, his intelligent face free of expression.

When William had finished Anthony turned to Saloman and asked. "May I enquire Mr Saloman, why you haven't already terminated the employment of the men who have been handling the redevelopment of these mines for you and preferably found them employment overseas? It would seem to me that they are the only witnesses that could be an embarrassment to you in a court of law. Presumably neither Trevylian nor his men would have been down these mines and unless the police have some corroboration from a witness, everything else would be surmise."

"Anthony, I don't think it is your place to question Mr Saloman's judgement," said William rapidly, frowning at him.

Saloman raised his hand to stop William, his eyes never leaving Anthony's. "No, let me hear what he has to say, he may have a point. Now, Mr Gladwell, why do you think it would be in my interest to arrange for these men to leave the State?"

Anthony dropped his eyes as he thought, then he looked at the older man. "It would seem to me that the nature of these ore deposits is exactly as you say. Nobody can ever look behind the exposed surface of the rock face to see what is there. Gold may be discernible on the surface or not, ore remaining loose in the workings may or may not contain gold in varying amounts. The only way that the police can succeed in bringing a case against you is to obtain an incriminating statement from one or more of the men employed by you to redevelop these mines. If the men are not in the State and preferably not in the country, I very much doubt that the evidence of the transport contractor would suffice. The police have surmised that the equipment carried in for you couldn't have dug out the additional new ore. I doubt that would be sufficient evidence to extradite a witness from another country. After all, what does it really matter to you if you haven't produced new ore, so long as what has gone through the battery has come out of that mine? I suggest that you give consideration to providing employment for these men outside this country, as I think the police will find it impossible to proceed with the case in their absence."

Saloman grinned, then leaning forward he squeezed Anthony's knee with a huge hand. "You are right, you young bastard, you're right." He exclaimed and laughed delightedly, his small eyes disappearing into the wrinkles at their sides.

****

Chapter 21
The other side of the tracks

The two young men paid off the taxi at the end of the bridge over the railway tracks then turned sharply into the dingy street and walked briskly along talking quietly together. Ahead a door opened and light streamed out. There was a babble of voices then the light was shut off as the door closed. Three men made their way down the front path to the gate and turned into the street talking together. There was a burst of raucous laughter and one of them started to sing:
"Charlotte the harlot lay dying,
a piss-pot supporting her head.
As she lay on the ground there, reclining,
this is what she said.
Take me back to the old family homestead
and bury me deep down below,
where the wedgetails and dingoes can't molest me
and the squatter's son..... sorry mate"
The carolling stopped in mid verse as the singer stumbled and fell against one of his companions and they both clung together for support while they found their balance. Then the trio were off again, their voices raised in unison, staggering along the street away from the two onlookers, the night made hideous by their song:
"The Parson's daughter she was there, the dirty little runt,
with poison ivy up her tail and thistles up the front,
singing who'll do it this time, who'll do it now,
the one that did it last time cannot do it now."
John Long frowned at the men weaving their way into the distance, then turned to his companion and drawled, "They look as though they've had enough to drink, Anthony. Down from the Goldfields no doubt."

"Probably," replied Anthony Gladwell with a shrug, "which reminds me that my respected uncle was none too pleased this afternoon when I gave Lew Saloman an easy way out of his dispute with the Gold Squad. My uncle never sees beyond the end of his nose. If we let the police get old Lew's gang into court, one of them would be sure to trip over his story and then in no time at all the whole lot would be singing."

"Yes, maybe," John said, as he stopped at the gate into the front garden of one of the terrace houses standing back from the street, "but William was expecting a long court hearing and that would have meant a fat fee for the firm. You really ought to know by now that profit is the main driving force in any business or profession. Cowan Dibney and West don't do anything for free."

"What rubbish you talk, John!" Anthony snorted. "Who has said anything about doing something for free. What we want is a partner on the board of each of Lew Saloman's companies. We should be offering a continuous legal service instead of providing him with occasional assistance like the fire brigade."

John turned and looked at his companion, considering what he had said. "Hmm! I see what you mean. It would certainly be worth considering. Let's forget all that for now and go in. You can then find out what old Lew wants to discuss with you, while I'll see what Mollie Craigie's girls can offer by way of short term relief."

He led the way up to the verandah and rang the doorbell.

When they were led into the brightly lit room at the rear of the house the first person Anthony saw sitting in an alcove at the far end was Lewis Saloman.

Dressed in a dark suit, the trousers of which strained across his huge thighs, the businessman laughed at something said to him by a pretty little brunette in a long dress of pale blue and silver. Raising a glass of beer, he drank it with relish. As he did so he caught sight of Anthony and beckoned him over.

A tiny birdlike woman of indeterminate age, with a sharp

featured face and dressed in a black velvet dress, advanced towards them. Mollie Craigie had come a long way from the day she had first gone on the streets in Melbourne. Subsequently brought to the west coast towards the end of the century when men out numbered women almost three to two, as one of a group of girls brought in to be employed in the first of Coolgardie's bawdy-houses, she had made every post a winner. Now she owned not only the freehold of this group of three terrace houses in Roe Street, which she had knocked together into one, but several similar businesses in Kalgoorlie and other mining towns on the West Australian Goldfields, as well as considerable other property including half a dozen hotels in Perth and Fremantle.

While content to employ a manager for each of her hotels it was to this Roe Street establishment that she gave the greater part of her personal attention, believing as she did, quite rightly, that this was the foundation of her business empire and the source of much of her considerable cash flow.

"Good evening gentlemen, it's good to see you. What would you like to drink?" she asked. Her eyes were as hard as agates as she stood there assessing them. She waved one of two heavily built men standing at the side of the room, forward to take their orders.

"Let me introduce you to two of our new girls. They have just arrived from the City of Churches, Adelaide of course." She beckoned to two girls sitting with others in a cluster near the piano.

The two young men ordered beer from the steward and Anthony, without waiting to be introduced to the girls, walked towards Lewis Saloman who greeted him with every appearance of friendliness, leaving Mollie Craigie staring with angry eyes at his back.

Bang! You're dead Anthony, thought John. You can't afford to offend Mrs Craigie and hope to develop a business of any size in this town.

After a moment Mollie turned back to John Long and made the formal introduction that she placed so much emphasis on, to ensure her clients felt at home. Then taking the other girl by the arm she escorted her across to where Anthony was talking to Saloman.

"Do you want to go over to where Mr Saloman is and join your friend or shall we sit over here by the window until the drinks come?"

John turned to the big blonde who had been introduced to him as Adele and regarded her quizzically.

"Whatever you like," he responded.

"I don't really mind, but Mr Saloman doesn't usually stay drinking for long. He'll want to go down to the rooms any moment now." She shifted her feet and stood with one hip out, in a gesture that was both awkward and oddly seductive.

He looked at her heavy figure and came to the conclusion that he would rather not talk to Lew Saloman. "Let's sit over there by the window," he said and he guided her to a small table with two hard chairs.

After a while Anthony left Saloman and came back through the press of men and their women partners who were now filling the room. He drew up a chair and sat down.

"Well, just as I said, old Lew wants me to go round and see him in the morning to discuss my ideas regarding his need for continuing legal advice." He grinned engagingly, very satisfied with his evening's work and looked at the blonde's décolletage, where her breasts were very much in evidence as she leaned forward towards John.

The small girl that Mrs Craigie had selected as a companion for Anthony came up and standing at his shoulder, leaned against him gently.

"I think the young lady is in need of some attention, Anthony," said John dryly.

Anthony started and looked up. "Oh, hello. I am sorry, I've forgotten your name, but I don't want anything to drink, do you? Can we go somewhere quiet?"

She nodded, still leaning against him, gently moving her body against his shoulder.

Anthony jumped to his feet nervously and excusing himself to John and the other girl, they walked off quickly through a curtained doorway.

The girl Adele laughed. "He's a jumpy little bloke isn't he? Is this the first time he's been here?"

"I think so, but a business deal always has a peculiar effect on him."

"Well I never," she murmured looking after Anthony. Then returning to business, she turned cow like eyes on John and leaned forward, her large breasts barely constrained by the deep plunging dress.

****

Chapter 22

There can be an unpleasant side to business

Martha placed the large oval meat dish containing the roast leg of mutton on the table in front of George's place and made sure that everything else was on the table; Aberdeen sausage made from minced mutton, bacon, egg and Worcestershire sauce; roast potatoes, crisp and brown; roast pumpkin, rich browned orange flesh with nutty flavoured grey green skin; tomato and onion pie in a deep round dish and thin sliced green runner beans from her garden.

She took off her apron and put her hands up to her hair to make sure it was in place, and sat down.

"George," she called in a high carrying voice. "The meal is on the table, would you come along please."

"You sound just as you always did, Mother." Anthony said kindly, taking out his napkin from its ring. "I miss your chivvying me now that I am living in Perth."

She smiled at her two younger sons, sitting quietly in their places.

Tim looked around the table, then spotted something missing and jumped to his feet. "We forgot the mint sauce, Mother."

"It's on the side, dear, in the glass jug." She watched him leave his place as her eldest son limped into the room from the sitting room and sat at the head of the table.

" Will you say grace please, Tim?" His mother asked.

They all bowed their heads as the youngest carried out the family's time honoured custom. "For health and strength and daily food, we praise thy name, oh Lord. Amen."

George commenced carving the mutton and passed the plates around the table for the others to load them with vegetables.

Anthony returned to the subject he had been talking about before they sat down.

"As I was saying, Mother, I bought shares in Saloman Timber and Trading. They can't go wrong because old Lew is guaranteed to make money out of this new timber contract. We have most of the independent sawmillers' production tied up and when the Government calls for bids for the supply of sleepers to the Indian Railways, the only bids will be from his companies. There will be nowhere else to go." He grinned mischievously as he passed his plate across to Tim to serve him with tomato and onion.

"What's got into you, Anthony?" asked George, laying down the carving knife and fork.

"I am Mr Saloman's legal adviser," he replied importantly. "I drew up the contracts with the sawmills. Tied them up tight, so they can only supply us."

"What happens if the sawmills want to supply sleepers to the Indian Railways themselves?" George persisted.

Anthony laughed. "They can't. We've agreed to take all their production in return for a firm undertaking that they will not supply a third party."

"But isn't that against the law, Anthony?" asked Martha quietly.

"No, they are individual contracts between a seller and a buyer. In any case in practice the law doesn't come in to it as they won't be making a complaint. Old Lew has one of his men at every sawmill and as soon as there is a sign that the sawmiller may be putting timber aside to ship to another party that man lets Lew know and he sends down a team of persuaders."

Martha stopped eating and looked at Anthony in horror. "Do you mean, that Mr Saloman has men who threaten the sawmillers?"

"Mother, it is in the interest of the timber industry to present a united face to these big contract buyers. They have to come to us to buy Jarrah sleepers; it's the best timber for the job there is.

It is hard and resists termites and so on. They use the offcut blocks in the streets of London; many famous streets there, like Lombard Street where the banks are, have been paved with Jarrah blocks. All we have to do is to make sure that the sawmillers understand that if we present a united front we will make more money."

George wiped his mouth on his napkin and looked across at his younger brother. "Which I suppose goes part way to explaining why we read in the West Australian newspaper of a fire at a sawmill. They aren't allowed to break away from the association with Saloman under threat of being put out of business. And you say this is not against the law. The contracts may not be, but what's arson? That's outside the law for sure."

Anthony's face darkened. "Our men don't threaten, they persuade. They point out the benefits of the contracts and the insurance this provides against the activities of people who may be tempted to set fire to mills that are undercutting the association's price, that's all." He glared at his eldest brother whom he privately regarded as unimaginative and therefore only suited to being a cocky farmer out here in The Dale.

Martha intervened. "That's enough you two," she said sharply. "I don't want you arguing on my birthday. Let's be happy together. We have George home at last from the war and I'm only sorry that Douglas is so busy in Adelaide and cannot come over and that Elizabeth couldn't be with us either today."

"I am sorry, Mother, it's my fault. Whether or not you like Mr Saloman he has been very kind and gone out of his way to give Tim a job as assistant farm manager on his property in the Berkshire Valley at Moora. You said you thought it would be good for him to have been able to go somewhere to be trained as a manager and I was very glad to have been able to arrange it." he sat back in his chair and looked around the table.

Martha hesitated. Yes, she thought, this is the sort of pressure that Mr Saloman puts on the sawmillers. Anthony is catching the habit from him.

You little sod, George thought, staring at Anthony in horror, as his younger brother sat in his chair looking around him smugly. Now you are leaning on Mother and you expect us all to stand to attention and salute by numbers, just because your greasy mate has given brother Tim a job where he can learn what you call proper farm management methods. Well, screw you lad, and the rest of your lousy city friends.

The Ford Model T swung through the big gates and chugged across the yard to pull up outside the door, above which a sign announced 'Office'.

Anthony Gladwell climbed from behind the wheel and looked around the open area in front of the warehouse. A pair of motor wagons loaded with bales of wool waited to be unloaded at the wooden ramp. A gang of men sweated with two-wheeled sack trolleys to push the big bales to the scales just inside the door for weighing and then into the building to be stacked.

Anthony straightened his tie and reaching into the front of the car, picked up his case. "Well, you know the way, O'Brien," he said and having adjusted his hat followed his thickset companion through the door.

They were ushered into a dingy office with yellowing plaster walls and dado height wood panelling. A small man of indeterminate age sat behind the desk and waved them to a pair of chairs opposite him.

"Good morning, Mr Snell," said Anthony and placed his hat on the edge of the desk. He opened his case and extracted a thick file tied with a pink ribbon.

"My name is Gladwell. You are already acquainted with Mr O'Brien."

Snell bobbed his head in a peculiar gesture, rather like Punch and completed the illusion by looking fixedly over Anthony's shoulder at something on the far wall. He sat there with his head on one side, saying nothing, while Anthony busied himself with undoing the pink ribbon. Laying out the file on the desk in front of him, Anthony looked up to find to his surprise that Snell was almost standing on his head with the effort to read the notes on the top sheet of paper upside down. Anthony closed the file and Snell sat down with a sigh of disappointment.

Disconcerted, Anthony picked up the file and opened it on his lap. He glanced at O'Brien who was sitting with his arms folded; then opened his mouth to speak.

Before he could do so however, the door creaked slowly open. He saw Snell's eyes lift and widen as they looked over his shoulder. Anthony felt the hair on the back of his neck stand up. He turned in his chair and looked behind him. As he did so a seemingly disembodied hand came around the door and was shortly followed by a head. Mr Snell breathed a sigh of relief as a slightly younger version of himself peered around the room through pince-nez. The intruder looked across the desk at Snell, bobbed his head, and withdrew. There followed a crash as something heavy hit the door. It swung wide and a large chair appeared and wiggled through the doorway then, held in front of the younger man, swayed into the room.

"Son ...Joe," mumbled Snell, whom Anthony now realised had omitted to put in his denture. "Put that bloody chair down over there," Snell roared in an enormous voice, rising from his chair and indicating a place against the wall at the end of the desk.

Snell sat down again in his swivel chair which contained a thick cushion to give its occupant more height. He pursed his lips, with the effect that his face looked like a burst paper bag and, returning his eyes to the back of the room bobbed his head again.

Anthony took this as a signal to carry on and trying to gather his thoughts cleared his throat. "Ahem, Mr Snell... Mr Saloman ...has asked me to come down to Fremantle to see you and to ..er ," he said haltingly. "request immediate payment of interest and principal on your loan which is subject to the contract I have before me." He finished in a rush.

Snell bobbed his head. "What's 'e want that for?" he demanded.

This time Anthony was ready. He spoke at length in somewhat pompous legal terms. "Under the terms and conditions of the contract, Mr Snell, you have agreed to pay interest at the rate of seven percent per annum on the sum outstanding; interest to be calculated and payable monthly. In addition you have agreed to pay one thousand pounds a quarter off the principal. You borrowed fifty thousand pounds against the security of these premises eleven months ago and while you initially paid both interest and principal promptly on receipt of Mr Saloman's monthly account, you are now five months overdue. In accordance with the terms of your agreement with Mr Saloman, he now demands full and immediate payment of the outstanding sum within seven days." He stopped, not sure what he expected Snell or his son to do.

Snell made no comment but continued to gaze over Anthony's shoulder at the far wall of the office.

Anthony looked behind him nervously, then glanced at Joe Snell, who was sitting bolt upright on the chair at the end of the desk making washing movements with his hands in front of him.

The silence was deafening.

Anthony caught Joe's eye momentarily but, like the proverbial blowfly it was off, flitting around the room before he could be sure that he had made contact.

Anthony raised his voice in an effort to obtain some reaction from the elder Snell. "Err...Mr Snell... I ....err...am instructed by Mr Saloman to tell you that you have not paid interest due on the sum you owe or reduced that sum by one thousand pounds at the last quarter day as is set out in the contract. You are therefore in breach of the contract. Under its terms, you must pay Mr Saloman the full sum you owe, plus interest owing to date, within seven days. If this is not forthcoming, Mr Saloman will go to court and seek an order that the property may be put up for auction and sold, and your debt settled out of the proceeds".

There was no response from either Snell, the eyes of both men were now studiously avoiding Anthony's while playing a game of chase all over the walls and the ceiling of the room.

Anthony tried again. "Mr Snell, the court will in my view, certainly grant a winding up order against your business and authorise the Public Trustee to conduct the auction and settle your outstanding debts." This time he hit pay dirt.

"Why?" Croaked the elder Snell, licking his lips.

Anthony went patiently through the situation again, ending up by asking for either a bank cheque for the sum outstanding or their acceptance of their liability and a signature on the letter he had prepared and had with him, agreeing to the auction of the property.

"But we paid 'is bill every month, didn't we Joe?" Snell said. Joe nodded his head vigorously.

"Stands to reason that we ain't goin' to pay her agin'." Snell leaned forward and the folds of his cheeks moved in the semblance of a smile, somewhat belied by his eyes.

Old Lew's never going to believe this, thought Anthony, remembering the foul mood Saloman had been in when Bull O'Brien had returned to the office empty handed the day before.

He waved his hand nonchalantly. "Mr Snell, you know as well as I do that Mr Saloman's office has not received the payments due over an extended period and that Mr O'Brien here has been calling at your office every week for the last two months seeking satisfaction under the terms of the contract."

Anthony sat back in his chair looking from father to son and wondering disdainfully how they had ever built a successful business.

Mr Snell was going red in the face. Anthony watched, fascinated, as he appeared to swell. Gripping the edge of the desk he rose to his feet.

Joe appeared appalled, "Nah Dad, 'ave a care. Don't let the little bastard rile yer." His voice rose to a scream as Snell rose to his full height and wrenching open the centre drawer of his desk he started rummaging in the contents.

"Now, Dad," Joe cried. "He'll apologise! You shouldn't cut him, Dad!"

Snell found what he was looking for with a cry of triumph and pulled out a wicked looking knife with a long blade.

Bull O'Brien leaped to his feet and shot through the door, slamming it behind him. The knife thudded into the door panel and stuck quivering.

Anthony sat riveted to the chair with fright.

Snell started to search again in his desk drawers, mouthing obscenities, the spittle running from the corners of his mouth, his eyes staring.

Joe leaped towards his father and putting his arms around him, tried to hold him. "Get out of here!" he shouted at Anthony. "Get out of here before he does you an injury."

Anthony grabbed his file and picking up his case and his hat ran from the room, past the clerks in the outer office and into the yard where he found Bull O'Brien cranking the Ford for all his worth. He leapt into the front seat.

The engine roared and Anthony let in the clutch and drove off as Bull flung himself onto the running board. Neither of them looked back as they went through the gate and turned into South Terrace. That was just as well perhaps as they may have seen the Snells, father and son, peering at them over the window sill of the office. Following the departure of the Ford from their sight, the Snells fell into each other's arms, laughing.

****

CHAPTER 23

Douglas comes up trumps

The scrape of the shovels rang above the continuous rumble of the mine. Water dripped from the rock above onto the three men who, sweating in the close atmosphere, shovelled the broken ore into the iron truck standing on the rails behind them.

They had come down the shaft that morning and walked to the working face at this stope where for the past few days they had been bogging out the ore that had been pushed down the shute from the level above.

The big man, O'Rourke, stopped and leaned on his shovel.

"Only got enough for another two trucks here young'un," he said, addressing the figure working beside him in the gloom. "We'll do it before we 'ave our scran."

The third man, a short Welshman, looked around him. "It won't be a moment too soon for me, boyo. I don't like the feel of this place. They're not leaving enough rock above us between the stope and the next level now that they are using them long drills and bigger charges."

O'Rourke scratched his head. What would you know about firing charges, you little gnome, he thought, you did all your mining in coal in the Old Dart and they don't fire that or the whole lot goes up, what with the black damp and all.

Aloud he said: "Stands to reason that the bigger the charge the more ground they can make and the more ore they can get out of the mine each shift. We've got a rule that they only fire at the end of the shift, when the mine is empty and the men up on the surface, so it's safe enough. Before they started to use the bigger charges we often ran out of ore before the shift was ended. I reckon it's reasonable."

"It's still too dangerous, man. They should 'ave left more

ground between the levels, 'specially where they've taken the lower levels further out and are now extending the workings above them. If they're not careful and leave plenty of pillars they're gunna collapse the whole lot."

"Dai! You talk a lotta crap," ejaculated the big man. "'How many times do I have to tell you, this is not a coal mine that's worked on a face. We're minin' Silver, Lead and Zinc and that's seam working.

Douglas Gladwell grinned to himself. He knew that in spite of their constant arguing they were good friends and that he was lucky to be working with them. After all it was only good luck that he had met the big Irishman when he came to Broken Hill at the end of his first year at Adelaide Medical School to work through the long summer vacation. Half starved he had been then, with no assistance from home except the occasional pound note that could be ill spared, pushed into a hastily scrawled letter from his sister Elizabeth.

He had fainted that first day underground from lack of food and the big man had picked him up and propped him against the side of the gallery in which they were working at the time. When he had come to it was Paddy O'Rourke who, recognising the evidence from personal experience, had shared one of his wife's big pasties with him. Learning that Douglas was planning to doss down for the night in his swag in the dry bed of the creek on the edge of town to save the cost of renting a room, Paddy had insisted on taking him home. There he had been given the use of an iron stretcher bed on the back verandah and a box in a corner of the back room used by the O'Rourke's four young boys in which to keep his clothes.

Every summer for three more years Douglas had been coming back to Broken Hill to earn enough to carry him through the rest of the year. Always he had stayed with the O'Rourkes and their six children, paying seven shillings and sixpence a week to Kathleen for his board and lodging. He was happy to walk to mass on Sunday with the family, a little girl on either side of him, as he told them the stories of Alfred the Great, King of Wessex, and his fight against the Danes in Somerset and Wiltshire that he had learned at his mother's knee.

The O'Rourkes had watched him develop from a quiet, shy boy into a mature young man, confident in himself and of his ability to master his chosen profession. They were proud that Broken Hill had been one of the first country towns in New South Wales to have electricity and were pleased that he could continue his studies when with them, often reading until well after midnight by the light of the electric light in their small kitchen. Young Doc, they called him, even though they knew that he still had to work for one more year at his studies prior to doing his clinical year and becoming qualified. He was so obviously more knowledgeable than they were regarding medicine. Kathleen had more than once taken the opportunity to browse through one or other of his books and had been both shocked and intrigued at what they contained.

Douglas picked up the bogging shovel and laying the blade flat on the rock floor of the stope, pushed it into the pile of loose rock, then turned and threw its contents into the iron truck. He fell once more into the slow steady rhythm that he was able to keep up for hours on end. He quickly reached the stage where he was able to divorce his mind from what he was doing and was able to go over the lectures in surgery that he had been attending during the past year.

Time passed rapidly and it seemed only a few minutes before he was aware that Paddy had called smoke-oh and the two older men had stopped work and gone down the tunnel to where they had put their lunch and the bottle of cold tea they drank with it.

He followed them down the tramway lines, his lamp lighting the black rock above and to each side as he trudged. He sat down beside his haversack that had been carried by some soldier in the AIF before it was sold him as a tucker-bag for two bob at the mine store. Opening the bag he took out the package that contained the food Kathleen had put up for him that morning; a mutton pasty for his lunch, a jam sandwich for morning smoke-oh and a piece of dark fruitcake for the afternoon break.

The older men lit pipes and puffed contentedly, leaning back against the rock wall. Douglas took a drink from the bottle, noting as usual that Kathleen had added a small quantity of sweet red wine to the tea, to give it a bit of body, she said. Paddy always had rum in his tea, but he didn't approve of a young man drinking spirits at his age. Douglas smiled. Paddy was always telling him that beer was the thing for a young man, not spirits that rot your guts.

He finished his scran and telling the others he needed to obey a call of nature, set off to the latrines beyond the junction of the stope with the main level.

He had just left the line of evil smelling seats and was adjusting his belt, when he was assailed by the tearing, shuddering rumble of a rock fall from up the stope where he had been working. The ground seemed to heave with the shock and putting his hand out to the wall to steady himself he felt it shake like a living thing. Pieces of rock fell out of the roof of the main tunnel and small stones seemed to run down the walls like grains of sand. After a while, the noise of the fall of loosened stone subsided. He could hear once again the usual noises of the mine, the air rushing through the ventilation trunk above, as it was pumped down to the working areas, the distant thud of the pumps that never stopped lifting the water out of the bottom levels and which, if ever they stopped for more than a few hours, would allow the ground water seeping down from the surface to flood the workings.

He ran forward and into the stope, where he stopped, unable to see as the air was full of dust. "Paddy, Dai, are you all right?" he shouted. There was no sound except for the dribbling of small stones.

Groping his way forward he stubbed his toe against a large rock and fell onto a heap of rubble. He picked himself up with difficulty, sat back on his heels and peered into the dust-laden air around him.

He scrambled forward up the heap until he had nearly reached the roof, then saw that more of the rock above appeared loose and about to fall. He called again. There was no response. Turning he made his way back to the main gallery and ran towards the shaft where there was a telephone box.

Arriving panting, he seized the handle of the bell generator and wound it madly. There was no reply so he cranked the generator again.

A voice complained. "Hang on a minute and I'll be with you."

Douglas could hear a faint conversation going on as, consumed with impatience he waited for a response.

At last a voice came on again. "Ullo! Ullo! Winding Room 'ere. What d'yer want?"

Douglas leaned forward and spoke into the mouthpiece fixed to the front of the instrument. "It's Douglas Gladwell speaking from level nine. There's been a bad fall in stope eleven and I reckon two men are under it." His voice wavered as the thought flashed through his mind of all those tons of rock crushing Paddy and Dai's bodies.

" 'old on lad," the tone of the voice had changed. "Just you wait there by the phone and I'll get the underground manager, 'e was 'ere just now." The line went dead.

Douglas waited in the faint illumination provided by the lights surrounding the cage entrance, a prey to his own imagination.

The shrill of the bell attracted his attention and he picked up the receiver.

"Ferguson here. Just tell me what happened, slowly," a voice said quietly.

Douglas took a deep breath and spoke as slowly as he could.

"Douglas Gladwell here, sir. I was working in stope number eleven with Paddy O'Rourke and Dai Reece. We were bogging out the stope and had only about half a truck to go. I came down to the dyke and as I was going back into the stope there was a rock fall. It shook the whole place. I ran in but it was full of dust and I couldn't see properly. There's a big heap of rock in the stope, about thirty yards up. I climbed up to the ceiling. It seems to completely block the tunnel. I called them, sir, but they didn't answer." The panic was rising in his throat again. "I'm afraid they are under the fall, sir. Please tell me what I should do now." His voice broke in spite of his efforts to remain calm.

"Just you stay where you are, young fellow. Stay beside the phone until we reach you. There has been a fall in level eight too. Most of the men of the mine rescue team are there. I'll come down with another team and we'll see what we can do."

Douglas heard the cage come down the shaft and stop at the level above. Then it passed him and went further down the shaft. He heard the doors open and close, before it finally came back to level nine where the doors opened and the underground manager and his shift boss came forward followed by seven or eight men of the mine rescue team.

"Gladwell, isn't it?" Ferguson asked, as the young man stepped towards them. "Come on then, you lead the way. Some of you men bring one of those trucks up. We'll need to have something to take away the debris."

When they reached the site of the fall the dust had already settled and they could see that the roof had collapsed and the tunnel was full of rubble, the tramlines disappearing into the fall.

"Right, we need props and lintels to shore up the roof. You, Jones and Pigott, get off and bring some up from the heap near the shaft. Cassidy, you help them and telephone to the surface and have more timber sent down."

Ferguson issued a string of instructions. The men attacking

the heap with shovels erected strong balks of timber and wedged them tight under the ceiling to stop any further movement. The work was slow and several hours passed, with the men working in relays, before they reached the iron truck still standing on the tram rails. It was crushed and leaning sideways. Half under the truck, his helmet on his head and partly protected by the remains of the truck, was the body of Dai Reece.

Douglas stepped forward and bending over him, felt for his pulse. He shook his head, then said in a business like voice. "There is nothing we can do for him. He's dead."

Ferguson looked at him. "Are you sure?"

"Yes, there's no pulse. Do you want to leave him here until the company doctor can see him?"

"No, he'll only be in the way and we must get to O'Rourke."

Douglas and one of the other men lifted the body out and, placing it on a stretcher, carried it out of the stope and into the gallery.

"You had better go up with him Gladwell and explain to the first aid people that I expect we'll need their help down here." Ferguson had followed them into the gallery.

"Sir, may I stay? I am in my last year of medicine at Adelaide and I could perhaps assist you here if you find Paddy is still alive. He's been a good friend to me and I would very much like to help, please."

Ferguson looked at him sympathetically. " All right, most of the first aid people are at level eight, so perhaps you had better remain here in case we find him before the doctor gets down here. Go with the stretcher now and leave Reece near the cage and telephone the winding room and ask them to send someone down to pick him up. Then come back here after they've taken him."

They found Paddy O'Rourke some time later, wedged in against the wall of the stope under a tangle of broken beams. The mass of wreckage was creaking under the weight of the roof and poised ready to collapse. There was just enough room for a small man to crawl in beside Paddy and Douglas wormed his way in to try to free him.

"Hello young'un, you better get back out of here before the whole lot comes down on us," whispered Paddy, who was lying on his back, his right arm free but broken, his left stretched out, trapped under a large rock that seemed to be carrying the weight from above.

Douglas ignored his advice. "Can you feel this arm?" he asked.

"No, its dead. I've got a rock sticking in me back that's hurting me much more,"

The timber moved, settling slightly and Paddy groaned.

"Hold it," Douglas shouted to the men in the tunnel above. "Don't shift anything, not just for a moment."

Someone shone a torch in under the timber.

Douglas said, "I'll have to explain to Mr Ferguson what the position is."

"Tell him to get the doctor and take this arm off, then you can get me out without bringing the lot down on top of us." Paddy whispered, sweat glistening on his forehead.

"Let us see about that, Paddy."

Douglas wriggled back carefully, getting to his feet as soon as he was clear of the wreckage.

Ferguson came forward. "How is he placed?" he asked.

Douglas beckoned him out of earshot of the man under the wreckage.

"He is lying in a sort of tunnel made up of timbers that are lying across him and onto a big rock that must have come down from the roof. His left arm is crushed by this rock and is holding him from moving. It's crushed flat and I doubt whether there is anything there that has not been pulped. The forearm disappears under the rock and he says he has no feeling in it at all. Paddy suggested that you get the doctor to come down and take his arm off and quite honestly I think it is the only thing to do. If we try to jack the rock and the wreckage up, apart from the risk of bringing the whole lot down on him, he'll probably bleed to death. Of course the shock may kill him too, but that is a lesser risk than losing him from loss of blood if the wreckage shifts further."

"I can't get a doctor. There is nobody available in the town for at least another two hours, they tell me. All we have are the first aid people. We'll just have to get a jack in there and try to lift the weight off of him. What do you think Cassidy, you've had plenty of experience of this sort of thing?"

He turned to the shift boss, standing silently beside them listening.

"Well, sorr. I don't rightly know. The way it is just now, oi'm proper frightened that we'll bring the whole damn lot down on 'im, not only the timber and rock that's there now, but half the roof too. It's very loose above where the shute was and it'd only take a bit of a shake and she'll slide and bury not only O'Rourke, but all the lads who are trying to get to him. In my view it would be best we don't try to lift it, if that can be avoided."

"Would you like me to amputate the limb, sir? I've done quite a few resections and I've no doubt I could do it." Douglas said quietly.

Ferguson studied the intelligent young face looking earnestly at him. "But you're not qualified yet, young fellow," he said kindly. "The powers that be would have you up in court."

"That's not important, sir. I know what to do and in any case if we don't get him out of there very soon, he is going to die."

"It is a terrible thing to have to do to your mate."

Douglas took this as approval and turning spoke briskly to the shift boss. "Cassidy, will you lend me that pocket knife of yours that you are always sharpening on Paddy's whetstone. I'll ask you for your thin leather belt Mr Ferguson, everyone else either uses a wide belt or braces to keep their strides up."

He put out his hand and collected both items from the two men who looked at him in horror.

"What about anaesthetic?" asked Ferguson sweating profusely.

"We'll needs do without." Douglas said shortly. He bent and picked up a steel rod that the men had been using as a probe in searching the rubble. "This will do to tighten the tourniquet."

Douglas turned to Ferguson and inspected his white shirt. "I'll be grateful if you would give me a piece of your shirt, Mr Ferguson. I'll need it for a bandage and you are the only person with a clean shirt just now."

Ferguson said nothing, but took off his waistcoat and pulling his shirt off gave it to Douglas who wordlessly ripped it into strips.

Having completed his preparations, he looked at the manager who was watching him closely. "I'll need some help to pull him out just as soon as I've cut him free, so please have someone follow me in," and he pushed the rough bandages into the front of his shirt.

Turning, he stepped forward and wormed his way back into the tangle of debris again.

"How are you feeling now, Paddy?" Douglas asked as he came up to the Irishman's head.

"Eh? Oh, it's you, young Doc. I'm awful cold, man. If they don't get a Doctor soon and take this arm off it's going to be too late, I'm right worried about what will happen to the kids and to Kathleen if I don't get out of here."

"The Doctor's held up, but we thought maybe I should do the job. It's pretty straightforward and I've done it before," he lied, thinking, well so I have if not on a living person.

"I couldn't care less who does it, as long as you get me out of here." Paddy lay there his eyes imploring, the sweat running down his face. "I'm not scared of you taking my arm off lad, it's just the thought of Kathleen being left with those kids to care for. Just fix it nice for me will yer."

"I'll do that Paddy. We're going to get you out of here, never fear. Just let me get around to the other side of you." Douglas moved over the injured man's body and slipping the leather belt under his arm twice, fastened it above the elbow. He looked down at his friend and said. "Now Paddy, I'm going to slip this rod in here and twist it into a tourniquet. It may hurt a bit, but I must do this or we can't get you out."

Paddy looked at him from a pain-ravaged face. "So I'll be the first real victim of your knife, Doctor Gladwell. You better make it quick as I can't stand this very much longer." He tried to grin but only succeeded in looking fiercer than usual.

Paddy shifted his shoulders trying to find a more comfortable place. "All right," he growled, closing his eyes. "Let the man see the rabbit."

Douglas positioned himself with his back to Paddy to keep him from seeing what he was doing and, having tightened the tourniquet and tied the steel rod firmly in place, he took up Cassidy's razor sharp clasp knife.

Then taking a deep breath, he cut into the sunburned skin of the powerful forearm in front of him to form a flap of flesh to cover the end of the bone. Paddy gave a groan and heaved once which nearly threw Douglas into the beam above him, then lay still. Without loss of time, Douglas cut rapidly down into the silver casing of the muscles, then around, severing the sinews and muscles before neatly cutting through the joint and finally the skin on the other side. He took the bandages from his shirtfront and wrapping them carefully around the stump, secured them neatly.

Turning he was surprised to find that the big Irishman was conscious, his tortured eyes looking at him through tears, his mouth bleeding.

Not wasting further time, Douglas looked towards the hole through which he had come and seeing Ferguson's face there asked him to pass him a rope so that he could fasten it around Paddy's chest.

Ferguson disappeared, returning with a piece of strong cord.

With infinite care they slowly drew Paddy out from under the wreckage. Douglas all the time behind him making sure the stump wasn't knocked as he instructed the manager and the men on the rope.

At last they had Paddy clear and, placing him on the waiting stretcher, took him to the surface. Douglas and Ferguson accompanied the stretcher in the cage and at the manager's suggestion Douglas went with Paddy in the waiting ambulance to the Broken Hill hospital.

Douglas didn't wait to talk to the hospital staff. As soon as they had placed Paddy on a trolley and wheeled him away into the operating theatre he secured a lift back to the mine.

It was difficult for Douglas to remain with Kathleen while Paddy was in hospital and though the Irishwoman certainly never blamed him for what he had done in his efforts to save her husbands life, it was clear that his continued presence in the house would only cause pain.

Much to his surprise Ferguson offered to accommodate him for the three weeks remaining before he returned to medical school, but he declined the kind offer and moved into a boarding house.

Douglas expected that there would be an enquiry and that he would have to face legal action for his unlicensed amputation of his friend's arm. However, though he had to attend the coroner's hearing into Dai Reece's death and to make a statement to the police regarding the circumstances of the operation, nothing was said officially.

The local doctor told him that his surgery had been excellent and that he had left ample skin and tissue for them to complete the job of providing a properly covered stump at the hospital. Apart from that professional opinion there were no further comments. Their workmates, being of the opinion that he had saved Paddy's life, were more interested in raising money for Dai Reece's widow and securing compensation for the accident and future employment on the surface at the mine for Paddy.

The day he caught the train across to Port Pirie and from there to Adelaide to resume his studies, he called at the hospital to say goodbye to Paddy.

He was stammering his thanks for their hospitality to Kathleen and Paddy at the latter's bedside, when Kathleen surprised him by getting up and kissing him, then giving him a small parcel.

"This is just a small present for you to remember us by, Douglas. It originally belonged to Paddy's mother and we would like you to have it."

He smiled at his friends shyly and left the ward unable to see clearly for tears.

Later, on the train that night, he opened the parcel and found it contained a leather bound copy of John Bunyan's 'A Pilgrim's Progress'.

In the flyleaf Kathleen had written:

"Young Doc,

May your labours bring you the happiness you deserve.

Always your friends,

The O'Rourke family."

****

CHAPTER 24
Elizabeth finds a mission

Elizabeth lay in bed on the side verandah of the rectory looking up at the underside of the corrugated iron roof while she listened to the hoarse cries of the butcherbirds in the garden.

She could see the small brown clay blisters on the rafters where the hornets had laid their eggs the previous summer and wondered how many of their grass green grubs had hatched out. Red ants were working their way busily across the stone wall of the house. Every now and again one would wander off to explore the other side of a stone and losing its way would panic and run around in ever increasing circles until it found the ant trail again. She smiled to herself. How like humans they were in this respect.

Elizabeth closed her eyes and dozed while in the background she could hear the early morning buzz of the insects from the garden, crickets clattering like so many castanets against the hum of bees.

When she awoke some time later it was to hear the rhythmic clank of a bucket handle, then the thump on the back verandah as her mother put down the milk. Elizabeth felt guilty to be dozing here in bed and turned her head to hear if her sister-in-law, Dorothy, George's wife of last year, was moving about yet.

Elizabeth had been shocked to hear Dorothy's scornful comments about the house and the inadequacy of the new bathroom, which she compared scathingly with that of her parent's home in West Perth, while George sat there nodding in agreement to everything his wife said. Wrinkling her nose in distaste she thought of Dorothy's unctuous voice the previous evening, when she had talked, sitting at the dinner table making no move to help with the dishes. "Dear mother,"

Dorothy had said, "you should retire from active participation in the farm work and move into York and enjoy yourself with your friends."

Elizabeth had been surprised when her mother had seemed to acquiesce to the idea and had little to say to the contrary. Ugh! Elizabeth shook herself; Dorothy made her flesh crawl with her pasty face and her prissy manners, though to be fair she did have some good points she thought, pleased to be able to put something on the other side of the equation. Dorothy could certainly cook like a dream, but whether George would be able to afford all the fancy things that she demanded, that was another thing altogether.

Elizabeth heard the galahs shriek as, disturbed, they rose in the air from the trees down by the gate onto the road. She could imagine the cloud of colourful pink and grey parrots lifting into the sky and circling around before descending again to roost in the cluster of sugar gums, survivors of the trees her mother had planted up the drive to the house when she had first come here. She had tended them so carefully, carrying water up from the river pool those first years when there was no other source of water available, only to see many die in the dry years immediately prior to the war when the river pool went salt.

The back gate banged and she heard someone crunching up the path, a man's stride. Oh Lord! Elizabeth said to herself, and I'm not dressed. She sprang out of bed and pulled on a warm dressing gown over her sensible winceyette night-gown with its high ruched neck and long sleeves. She ran her hands through her hair then bent to make the bed. Once that was done she rushed along the verandah and into the bathroom built off the corner of the house.

Brushing her teeth, she looked into the mirror on the wall over the wash bowl and noted once again the grey hairs that were beginning to show here and there amongst her thick brown hair. She grinned at her vanity. After all, she thought, a lecturer at the University of Western Australia could expect to have a few grey hairs by the time she was twenty-nine, especially as this lecturer had recently been awarded her doctorate, the thesis for which she had completed while still carrying a full teaching load.

When she entered the kitchen five minutes later, there was not a hair out of place her white broderie anglaise blouse was crisp and fresh over a sensible blue worsted skirt.

Her mother swung around from the wood stove and smiled at her.

"Good morning dear," she said. "I've just had Peter Sievright to see me. I wonder whether you would like to come down with me to Dora's after breakfast. Apparently Fred has had another bad night and Peter wants me to talk to Dora and try to persuade her that he could manage very well by himself if she and Fred were to move into Beverley. I've told him I would because I know how much it concerns Dora when they are out here on the farm and Fred has one of these turns. If they were in town the doctor would be handy and in any case one of the sisters at the hospital could always help her in an emergency."

"How is Peter, it's a long time since I saw him last?" asked Elizabeth.

Martha Gladwell pursed her lips, her head on one side as she considered this question. "He has almost entirely recovered from the injury to his arm and of course I never notice the scars to his face. He is terribly shy and inclined not to want to meet strangers nowadays. It really is a shame as he is a very decent man and so kind not only to Dora, but also Edith and me. He has always been particularly thoughtful and considerate towards others who lost boys during the war, especially Clara Webb and Charlotte. I just wish we had someone like him in parliament instead of braggarts like Saloman."

"Mother, why do people always want to reorder everyone else's life?" Elizabeth asked. "Dorothy is so certain that you would be happier elsewhere. Is she expecting a child?"

Martha smiled. "My dear, Dorothy will never have a child. She is physically incapable of having one, which is just as well as George cannot give her one. As you know, we are very lucky to have George with us today, he went right through the war and was wounded twice and, though he was back in the trenches within four weeks, the second injury affected his ability to have children. When the war was over and they returned to England to await transports to bring them back to Australia, the soldiers were in such a poor state of health that they went down like flies during that awful influenza epidemic. George was in the military hospital at Sutton Veny for weeks, where over a hundred died, including doctors and nurses. It's such a pretty village and quite close to Warminster where I was brought up. George always says that the local people were wonderful to them, in particular my sister, your Aunt Ailine."

"Oh, well, that explains a lot," said Elizabeth thoughtfully. "I can understand you being willing to leave the farm for George to run, now that Tim is at Moora. Perhaps they will adopt a child, but what would you do, have a trip to England and go and see Aunt Ailine? What about Arthur Trevylian? He has been so kind to us. Have you heard from him recently? When he and that other man were working out here when I was little I always thought he was rather keen on you."

"Hush child," admonished her mother and she smiled as at a secret joke.

When Elizabeth and Martha arrived at the Sievrights' house, they were surprised to find that Dora had set up the tea table on the lawn under the old pepper trees on the river side of the house.

"This looks fun," said Martha, as carrying a tray she followed Dora around the verandah.

As the ladies approached the table both men stood up and Peter came around to take the tray from Martha so that she could spread a cloth.

"Hello Peter, I haven't seen you for such a long time." Elizabeth said cheerfully, noting that from this side his face appeared untouched and was rather good looking.

As he turned his head towards her he brought the scarring on the other side of his face into view.

"Oh, hello Elizabeth," he replied easily. "I heard that you had completed your doctorate. Congratulations. You must be pleased it is done as it would have meant a tremendous amount of extra work. No wonder you are looking tired. You had better stay up here for a while and put some flesh on your bones. The rectory is a good paddock you know."

She laughed as she put down the plates on the table. "I know that I'll be as fat as a whale if I keep eating morning teas."

"Rubbish!" Fred Sievright joined in the raillery. "You are like your mother, my dear, you never keep still for an instant. Not that you wouldn't be improved if you had a little more fat on your hips. What do you think, Pete?"

Peter stood his head on one side and looked her up and down, stroking his chin with one hand, a caricature of a livestock buyer at the local market.

"Actually, I quite like the lean and hungry look myself, Dad. It's all the rage with these modern young flappers, long legs, lean rump, only thing that I don't like is the flat bosomed bit. Not that Elizabeth suffers in that respect. Yes, come to think of it, she could look a lot worse."

Elizabeth flushed and her head came up to administer a sharp rebuke. As she lifted her eyes to Peter's she was surprised to see a look of extraordinary tenderness that gave him an appearance of great charm in spite of the damage wrought by his wounds.

"Your problem is that you don't get the opportunity out

here to see all the talent that is on offer," she rejoined, not wishing to let him get away with it entirely.

"Pouf ! You don't know what we see passing by. Vicky and Sally Webb often drive down this road and though Vicky has given up playing the field since she retired to be a married woman, it still doesn't stop her from giving me a wave whenever she sees me. Sally of course is still chasing after John Lejeune. However I am optimistic that at any moment now, she'll realise the futility of that pursuit and will remember me, even if I am nearly old enough to be her father. But here, I'm forgetting my manners and Mum is giving me her look, so you sit down on this chair."

He held a chair for her as she sat down and then took the one next to her.

The conversation was lively and Elizabeth was glad to be among friends at Bolumbygine again.

"Have you seen Charlotte recently, Martha?" Dora enquired of her friend.

Martha had been sitting quietly watching Elizabeth laughing with Peter and Fred. She didn't immediately respond, then turned to Dora, who she thought was looking very much older these days, even though she still carried herself beautifully.

"Not since Easter," she replied. "Charlotte was telling me at that time how glad she was Vicky had married that young solicitor. I am not so sure that she will be so pleased now that old Mr Webb left a large part of his interest in Broughton Park to the two girls, and Vicky's husband has persuaded her to ask to be paid out."

"Oh dear!" Dora's mouth dropped. "I am surprised that Charles Webb didn't entail the property in some way, but having lost the three boys it would be difficult to know what was for the best. He would have hated to have Broughton pass out of the family. Wherever will Harry and Charlotte find the money to buy the girls out? Perhaps they will sell the property as they only have the two girls to live for now, though there is always the possibility that John Lejeune could be interested. In the property I mean." She smiled.

"I really don't know Dora. Charlotte had been hoping against hope that one of the girls would marry a farmer. Now Vicky is married to a lawyer and Sally is such a flipperty sort of lass. I know what you are thinking. Sally has always been dangling after John Lejeune, but he is spending more time in the Gascoyne since he bought that station near Carnarvon. The thing is, you can't play God when you leave your children property and see into the future. Clara Webb has no direct male descendants other than Harry, and I don't suppose she saw any need to interfere."

"What does Elizabeth say about it?" Dora persisted, looking towards the slim young woman laughing happily with Peter and Fred.

Martha turned and looked in their direction.

"Nothing," she said quietly, with some pride. "She is very loyal to the Webbs and so she should be after all the kindness they have given her over the years."

Really Dora, she thought, this is most unlike you and not your business. Aloud she called: "We must go Elizabeth, I have to get lunch," she smiled a Dora. "I have a few problems of my own just now, particularly Dorothy, as you would understand. However there is one piece of good news; Douglas is returning to West Australia next week. He is going into general practice in Kalgoorlie. The Managing Director of one of the larger mines, a Mr Ferguson, who knew him when he was working at Broken Hill in the summer vacations, has offered him the position of company doctor. That will give him a good start."

Dora smiled, "That's wonderful news, you must be pleased."

They both stood and started to collect the crockery onto the tray.

Dora said quietly, " I saw Dorothy the other Sunday at Church. Is she by any chance pregnant?"

Martha stopped short and looked at her. "I don't think so, I am sure that I would have noticed, but then I do see her every day and she has an unfortunate figure. In any case I would be the last to know. She is very secretive and would never tell me."

"That's sad, Martha."

"Yes, though I tell myself that is one problem I never had. My mother-in-law only visited me twice in my married life. We were left to sink or swim, I can tell you. What I should do now is to go off and leave George and Dorothy to get on with their lives. Perhaps that is what I will do, too!"

Martha picked up the tray and having said goodbye to Fred and Peter, she walked determinedly towards the house followed by Dora and Elizabeth.

Elizabeth continued to stay with her mother, to the increasing concern of her sister-in-law. Dorothy in fact became convinced that she was planning perhaps to take up permanent residence and said as much to George. He assured her, however, that as soon as the university year recommenced Elizabeth would be gone. This confidently expressed assertion did little to assuage Dorothy's worries and she persisted in making suggestions that Martha would be happier living in Beverley or York.

Martha's answer to this was to smile and agree that it would be a project she would consider if a suitable house became available.

Dorothy did her best, going into town with George in their new Dodge motor car and coming home with details of all the houses that were for sale. Martha for her part went through all the papers and though she was apparently most happy to discuss the details with them, she very adroitly found good reason to avoid Dorothy's often repeated suggestions to make a day with the local agents to inspect any of them.

Tim came down from Moora where he had now taken up a

large parcel of good grazing land to the east of the town. He fanned the flames of dissension by suggesting in front of the whole family that his mother should go up there and keep house for him.

Martha thanked him kindly and to Dorothy's chagrin declined, saying that she had promised their father she would stay on the farm until all the children were settled. She indicated that she would discuss the matter with Douglas when he arrived and then would decide what to do.

Elizabeth was thinking of these events as she walked up to the rectory from the little church where she had been helping Dora with the flowers. Coming to the trees at the gate she was surprised to see Peter standing at the side of the road in earnest conversation with a horseman who had his back to her.

Glancing up, Peter saw her and waved. The horseman turned and Elizabeth recognised John Lejeune, whom she hadn't seen in an age.

"Hello! It is Elizabeth isn't it?" he said as swivelling in his saddle, he stared at her.

"Hands off John. That's my girl," laughed Peter. "She knows your reputation too well to be taken in by your pommie charm."

John smiled, showing his white teeth. "Well, you're a dark horse, Peter. I thought you had retired from the field and now you are warning me off the best looking filly in the district. You can get lost, lad."

Elizabeth came up to them blushing, but with her head held high.

"Well, Mr Lejeune, what brings you over the hill today? You don't usually come this way. I always understood that you went down the river and across to York."

"So I do, there is usually nothing on this side to attract me. I just came over to discuss a matter of mutual interest with Peter. However that is my good fortune because if I had known that Miss Elizabeth Gladwell, hold it, shouldn't it be Doctor

Gladwell now?" He looked at her enquiringly as she blushed furiously. "Yes, of course that is right, isn't it? Someone or other told me you had received your doctorate. Congratulations. At any rate Doctor, if I had known that you were here, I would have been coming this way daily."

She laughed up at him. "I have never heard so much rubbish in my life, though I am very pleased to see you. How is your brother, is he still in England?"

John explained that his brother Robert was married and living with his wife and their children on the family farm in Essex. Then excusing himself, he lifted his hat to Elizabeth and turning his horse away, trotted up the road towards Myuna.

Peter stood quietly looking after him until he had disappeared among the trees, then turned to Elizabeth and took her hands.

"You shouldn't take any notice of John," he said earnestly, looking into her eyes. "He may be a terrible flirt but there is no harm in him and he has never been the wild man that Robert was. Since he returned from the war he has been a good friend to me and, believe me, he's as straight as a die."

Elizabeth looked at him, making no attempt to disengage her hands. "You are probably right, I've never known him well. To me he has always been one of those marvellously polished Englishmen that one occasionally meets who understate everything and never show their feelings. I always feel they're cold fish. Funnily enough, Mother would probably agree with you. She says that they are shy and a little withdrawn but underneath it all they feel things passionately." She paused and wrinkled her forehead. "Now, I wonder how she came to that conclusion. I am sorry that I didn't know my father better, Peter. He always looked something like a Spanish brigand to me."

"I'm unable to help you there, my dear. I hardly knew him. He always seemed to be rather inclined to look down on people like us. I am sure he was very good at what he did for the people of his parish as he was much missed. However, it was always your mother whom we loved. She was such fun, always laughing regardless of the difficulties she faced. It was not at all easy for her when your father died, Elizabeth. Most women would have dropped their bundle when they found themselves left with six small children, no income and if the Church had had its way at the time, they would have probably thrown the lot of you out of the rectory while they installed another man there. Mum has always said that it was your mother's sheer guts that impressed old Charlie Webb enough to get him to go and see the bishop, and that really saved the day. You know something Elizabeth, you are very like your mother, you have the same strengths, tenacity of purpose and application."

"Have I, Peter?" she murmured, fearing to disturb the direction his thoughts were taking.

He looked at her, the scar across his forehead and down his cheek standing out against the tanned skin.

"No, you are not like your mother," he said quietly. "People only say that because they love and respect her and you remind them of the qualities they see in your mother. You are your own generous self, Elizabeth. Your mother was never beautiful and you are."

He pulled her gently towards him and almost without realising it was happening, she came into his arms.

****

CHAPTER 25
Kalgoorlie, 1925

The smartly dressed, grey haired woman stood at the counter in the drapery department of the store in Hannan Street, Kalgoorlie, and waited for the saleswoman to return.

Holding her handbag in both hands before her, Martha Gladwell looked up at the placard advertising 'Milwards needles, finest sharps, straws and crewels. Made in England.' She smiled as she remembered going with her mother to buy needles and thread in Warminster as a child, walking up Market Street in early winter and into the Market Place, where cattle were tied to iron rails along the pavement, their breath steaming in the cold, the sheep penned outside the Bath Arms, their amber coloured eyes and oval pupils oddly staring as they peered at her from between the split withes of the hurdles. Back again on the other side of the street, they passed the Old Bell and went into the grocers, a wondrous shop full of smells to tickle any little girl's nose. Out into the street again, followed by the odour of fresh roasted coffee, they looked at the big shire horses, their carts loaded with bags of grain standing along the street, waiting patiently for the corn merchants' buyers. In the echoing corn market under its iron pillared roof, men moved between the heaps of grain, sampling, discussing the weather and its possible impact on prices of farm produce.

"Martha Gladwell, if my eyes are to be believed," said a well remembered voice with a broad accent, "and not changed one jot."

Martha jumped and came out of her reverie with a rush, not sure whether the voice was in her daydream or not. She looked wildly about her, then caught sight of the burly figure standing beside her.

"Arthur!" she gasped. "Arthur Trevylian. What are you doing here? No, of course I understand, you have business interests up here haven't you?"

Arthur nodded, his kind eyes smiling at her from under eyebrows flecked with grey.

"I heard the other day that you had come up here to live with your son, the doctor." He smiled his eyes twinkling. "I've been trying to pluck up courage to call on you this past week, but I hardly expected to find you in one of my stores."

"Oh! Do you own this shop?"

He shrugged, "Yes, unfortunately, because I don't know very much about retailing. I am not a storekeeper by inclination and prefer other ways of making a living. I leave the manager here to look after the business in his own way, just as long as he provides me with a reasonable return on my investment. But tell me about the family, Martha, how are Elizabeth and the boys?"

Martha explained that Elizabeth was planning to marry Peter Sievright in the spring and would be living on the Sievright's farm; that George and his wife were now at the rectory while Tim was farming near Moora. She thanked him once again for his kindness and assistance over the years when the family had been struggling.

"Don't talk about that, I did little enough," he said gruffly. "Let's talk about something important. What about Anthony, what is he doing?" he enquired. "I heard he had left Cowan, Dibney and West and has been working for Lewis Saloman. What do you think of that?" he looked at her keenly.

Martha made no reply and he thought he could detect pain in her eyes.

"No, don't answer," he said kindly. "Saloman is no friend of mine, though I did think his idea of having his own lawyer on his staff was clever and typical of the man. I wondered whether Anthony would be interested in joining me. I have heard that he doesn't exactly enjoy his role as chief debt collector for old

Lew and thought Anthony may be wondering whether he would be better off sticking to the law rather than doing Lew's dirty work for him."

Martha lifted her head and looked at him. "I've never been happy that Anthony is associated with that man, Arthur, and while Anthony would not take it kindly if I tried to tell him how to manage his affairs, he did tell me that he had approached a friend seeking a place in a law practice recently. If you were to speak to him, you may find him receptive to any proposal you may care to make."

"I'll do that Martha, because I have always had the highest regard for his intellect, as did the staff at the University. There is no harm in him. What he really needs is a steadying hand. He'll not get that from Saloman I am afraid."

The saleswoman now returned and addressed Martha.

"I am sorry madam," she said briskly, well aware who Arthur was. "We haven't anything like that material in stock. The traveller for the importers will be up next week and if you care to let me know the length you need and leave the sample with me, I'll ask him whether he can secure it from somewhere in Perth if they haven't got it in stock themselves."

"That would be kind of you." Martha agreed and completed her instructions.

Turning to Arthur, who had remained standing quietly beside her, she looked up at him and smiled serenely.

"Arthur, would you care to come over for tea on Sunday?" she asked. "Douglas will be there, though I know he has made arrangements to go down with his trainer to see his new race horse a little after three o'clock, so we wouldn't be disturbed and could have a good talk about old times."

Arthur accepted her invitation and escorting her to the door walked outside with her.

"Well, Arthur," she said, giving him her hand. "I am so glad to see you again. Now don't forget, Sunday at around three. Come early please as I am looking forward to hearing all your news." She looked up at him and was surprised to find he was smiling down at her, a most peculiar look in his eye.

Disconcerted, she pulled her hand away from his and turning walked rapidly up the street.

"Hey, Martha," Arthur called after her. "You're going the wrong way. Don't you go that way?" he pointed in the other direction. "I thought you lived down there towards Boulder Road."

He grinned broadly as he saw her check, then turn and dodging the traffic crossed the road and start back on the other side, marching along, her head in the air pretending she hadn't heard him. As he watched her trim figure go by she shyly waved to him over her shoulder before continuing on her way.

He remained watching her until she passed out of sight.

"That's a fine young chap", Arthur said, leaning back in the cane chair on the back verandah of the house overlooking the shaded garden.

"Yes," agreed Martha, "he has always been a hard working boy, even though he was the most mischievous of them all and always in minor troubles at school."

"Nice garden here, Martha!"

She laughed. "Yes, it is. As you would probably know, the last doctor who had this practice had two mistresses, both of whom lived with him at the same time. The only way he kept the peace in the house, or so Douglas tells me, was to give one the task of caring for the house and the other the garden to look after. As a result both areas of responsibility were immaculate. I was most impressed when I came here and Douglas showed me round."

Martha smiled at him as she rocked in the old chair she had brought with her from the verandah of the rectory.

"What happened to Billy Pederick?" she demanded suddenly. "Where is he now? I know you severed your business partnership with him just before the war."

Arthur looked serious, "He died at Gallipoli in 1915, at Walker's Ridge, I believe."

"I am sorry to hear that, I didn't know," she said gently. "Did he leave any family?"

"No, he never married."

She looked pensive. "The first time I saw him, I thought he was quite dangerous. Later I realised that he had a heart of gold. It was just that he had been drinking on the first occasion."

"But you never saw him the worse for drink, Martha. He never drank when we were out on the farm with you," he looked at her closely.

"Oh, yes I did, and you too," she asserted firmly. "I saw you both rolling drunk at the Freemasons Hotel at Albany, where this chair came from, the first night I spent in this country in ninety-two. In fact Billy tried to interfere with me, out on the back verandah upstairs on the first floor of the hotel. It was the first time I ever hit a man."

He looked at her in amazement. "Don't tell me that you're the girl who got married in Albany and Billy took such a shine to, she certainly belted him one that night."

"Yes, I know I did. Not that I was very proud of it." She laughed at the expression on his face. "But that was nothing to what I did to him at the York Hospital some years later."

His mouth dropped, then he recovered himself. "Martha, I didn't know that was you either. Come to think of it, Billy always thought he had met you somewhere. He was quite certain of it when we first came out to Bolumbygine. I couldn't work out where he could have met you."

"Didn't Father O'Mear tell you that it was my husband that died in the York Hospital the night Bill Pederick brought you in to have that cut in your head stitched?" She pointed to the scar on his forehead.

"No, he never did." Arthur was aghast. "Well, next time I see Bishop O'Mear, I'll ask him what he was about," he added fiercely.

"Oh, he knew all right, though he may have thought you would have been embarrassed if you had known that Robert's death could have been attributed in any way to the noise that Bill Pederick made. Not that Billy had any understanding of the reason we had to keep Robert quiet that night," she nodded. "Well, that explains quite a lot. Of course I never mentioned the subject to you, but why did you stay on, helping me on the farm, when I couldn't pay you? I always thought it was because you felt guilty about that night in York."

"Good grief, no!" he exclaimed. "It was nothing to do with that. We came out as we said to have a break and then I stayed on because I had fallen in love with you and had hopes you would marry me if I hung about for a while."

Startled, she said softly. "Arthur Trevylian! What did you think I was, a ripe plum ready to fall off the tree into your hands?"

He looked into her eyes. "No, you certainly made that clear when you ran away from me the day I asked you to come with me and bring the kids."

"You could have come after me, you know. If you had, I would have changed my mind, perhaps!"

He jumped to his feet and stood looking down at her.

"Well, then!" he cried. "What's stopping you now?"

"Why, nothing that I know of." Martha looked up at him provocatively.

Taking her hands, he pulled her to her feet and folded her in his arms.

"Then let's not waste a moment of the time left to us, my dear," he growled, then kissed her.

****

Colin Price